THE GREEN VAULTS

JOACHIM MENZHAUSEN

THE GREEN VAULTS

PHOTOGRAPHS BY

GERHARD REINHOLD

EDITION LEIPZIG

TRANSLATED FROM THE GERMAN BY MARIANNE HERZFELD AND
REVISED BY PROFESSOR D. TALBOT RICE
WE ALSO WANT TO THANK MRS. R. GAZE FOR HER ASSISTANCE

DESIGN BY HORST ERICH WOLTER, LEIPZIG
PRODUCTION BY DRUCKEREI FORTSCHRITT, ERFURT
COPYRIGHT 1970 BY EDITION LEIPZIG
LIC. 600/91/70
PRINTED IN THE GERMAN DEMOCRATIC REPUBLIC

CONTENTS

PREFACE

The Green Vaults is one of the richest treasuries in Europe. Its unique setting, dating mainly from the early eighteenth century, was more famous than that of any other. A considerable part of this decoration was destroyed towards the end of the Second World War. What remained is being restored.

The Collection in the Green Vaults is one of the most outstanding of its kind because of the number and variety of the objects it contains. There are more than three thousand one hundred works made of gold, silver or precious stones, of almost every kind of semi-precious stones, of ivory, amber, ceramics, mother of pearl, of coconut or ostrich egg, of enamel, bronze, iron, wood or glass. There are objects of first-rate quality in each of these groups and hardly any that are of inferior quality as works of art.

The most recent publication on the Collection is "*Das Grüne Gewölbe zu Dresden*" by the late Director Jean-Louis Sponsel, four volumes, published at Leipzig between 1925 and 1932. It is of fundamental importance as a summary of the hundred years of research done by the men in charge of the Collection and as the result of the splendid work performed by Sponsel on the contents and the history of the Dresden treasury. Neither in its scope nor in its conclusions does the present book seek to emulate this work or to displace it: it has been written to satisfy the growing interest shown in the Green Vaults by an ever-increasing number of visitors.

But its publication is also justified by the time and the events that separate it from Sponsel's four volumes and it endeavours to make available the knowledge that has been acquired during the last forty years about some of the works of art in the Collection. The restricted space available in the catalogue has demanded extreme conciseness. Besides it has been possible to shed a new light on the history of the treasury, though this was in fact particularly difficult because of the destruction of the old rooms of the museum and the loss of the library, card indexes, and so forth. This book therefore is proof of the work done by all those who have been working for the Green Vaults since its treasures were returned by the Soviet authorities in 1958 from safe-keeping in the Soviet Union.

THE EARLIEST ARRANGEMENT OF THE COLLECTION

In 1721 Augustus the Strong, Elector of Saxony and King of Poland, gave orders that a certain room of about 90 square metres on the somewhat elevated ground floor of the Dresden Palace should have an opening made in its northern wall to make it accessible from the adjoining hall. Both windows of the room were secured by strong lattices and iron shutters. There was an outer wall of 2.5 m. in depth and three inner walls each of 1.5 m. The room was vaulted as were all the rooms in this part of the west wing of the Palace. Until then the only access to the room had been by way of a spiral staircase concealed in the thickness of the inner wall; it led to the private apartments of the Prince. This staircase was now walled up, as the room was to be put to another use. Its walls had originally been painted green; a fact discovered recently when portions added in the eighteenth century were taken down for restoration, and some bits of the rough-casting, dating from the sixteenth century, were exposed to view. The descriptive name "Green Vaults" (sometimes spelt "Green Vault") for these rooms had very probably been used colloquially by the inhabitants of the Palace ever since this part of the building had been completed in 1554; the name appears in a document of 1572 for the first time (1).

The Secret Deposit and the "Green Vaults" The oldest Core of the Collection The Exhibition Rooms and their Decoration The earliest Description of the Green Vaults.

Officially the room was named "The Secret Deposit" in accordance with its function. It was the treasury of the Electors of Saxony. Reserves of money, jewellery, precious works of art and important official documents were stored there. As in all treasuries, the contents of the Green Vaults did not remain permanently the same, but changed through the course of years. In 1629 Philipp Hainhofer, a diplomat and art-dealer from Augsburg, came to Dresden to ask the Elector John George I to support the hard-pressed Protestant party of Augsburg. He wrote in his report on the journey: "This Elector, like his noble forbears, coins good money, beautiful new, broad, large Thaler of the same kind as those of the Elector of Bavaria. Many thousands of them are deposited in the beautiful treasury, where you find side by side with vessels of silver, others of solid gold, of precious stone or of crystal; several millions in gold are hidden there."

We do not know for certain whether Hainhofer had been admitted to the Secret Deposit, but it may well be correct that vessels of precious stone were kept there at that time, that is a few years before the famous Pavilion on the Jungfernbastei in Dresden was decorated with them. This may be why the inventories of 1610 and 1640 of the Cabinet of Curiosities (*Kunstkammer*) enumerate only a few of these valuable works of art.

Apart from Hainhofer's report there is only the inventory of 1588 to provide information about this room: in six cupboards there were blocks of ore, small caskets made of gold or silver, objects of amber, silver-gilt vessels and sixty vessels of rock crystal. Some of the most beautiful and valuable vessels of rock crystal extant today belonged to this original collection. We know of occasional additions and disposals made in the course of the seventeenth century, but it is certain that works of art of the kind that are exhibited in the Green Vaults at present were always stored in the Secret Deposit. The Green Vaults therefore forms the basis of the present-day museum in three respects: it gave it its name, formed part of its home and contained works of art which constitute an essential portion of its collections today.

In 1721 three rooms were selected to serve specific purposes: the Secret Deposit became the "Silver Room", the neighbouring hall became the "Hall of Preciosities", and the third room became the "Jewellery Room". These three rooms of the treasury were to represent an entirely new kind of collection: a museum. Until then the treasuries of princes, towns, temples and churches had from earliest history been closed repositories, well guarded and secured, to which the owners alone and some chosen official persons had access. A constant watch was kept over these hidden treasures belonging to social groups or to those who were to control them: they contained monetary reserves for times of need, works of art and objects regarded as sacred on historical or religious grounds, as well as others symbolizing the might of their owners. The transformation of a Secret Deposit into a collection for exhibition is one of the many innovations and far-reaching changes which took place in the eighteenth century and are still of importance today. It was another century, however, before the treasuries of the other princely houses of Europe and of the principal churches began to equip themselves with show-cases and opened their doors to the vast numbers of those who are interested in art and research or merely eager to gaze.

There were special reasons for this innovation at the Court of Saxony, but before dealing with them, it might be better to provide some information about the origin of the treasures which filled these three rooms. The monetary reserves and the secret papers were of course stored elsewhere, and what was left of the valuable objects from the Secret Deposit was insufficient to spread out over all three rooms.

The room where the jewellery was to be kept was the first to be finished. An inventory of it survives in the Green Vaults signed by Augustus the Strong on 8th June 1722. It states: "In obedience to Our order, given by word of mouth, all

Our jewels, which until now We had kept under Our own lock and key, have been brought to the so-called Green Vaults of the Palace, to be stored there safely in the large cupboard specially made for the purpose; this present complete and correct inventory, plus appendix, consisting of one hundred and forty-one pages, has been made, shown and handed over to Us by Count Vitzthumb, Our privy councillor." The first eighty-six pages of this inventory enumerate jewellery sets made of silver, gold, agates, cornelians, emeralds, rubies, sapphires, diamond-rosettes and brilliants, most of which are still extant. On pages eighty-seven to ninety-two follows a list of single pieces of jewellery and of reserves of non-set pearls and precious stones, while pages ninety-three to one hundred and forty-one, entitled the appendix, record various additions to and disposals of parts of the sets. This collection of jewellery, until then in the personal safekeeping of the monarch, was estimated at 3,402,548 Thaler by the Court Jewellers *Johann Melchior Dinglinger* and *Johann Heinrich Köhler* and the Court Agent *Jonas Meyer*.

The next inventory was signed by Augustus the Strong on 30th June 1723; it is that of the Silver Room in the former Secret Deposit, and is entitled: "Inventory of the vessels made of solid gold, of silver gilt, silver or silver alloy, stored in the Royal Green Vaults". On two hundred and seventy-three pages it describes utensils, vessels and figures made of precious metal, all arranged in groups, numbered and with their weight given. Some of these objects are still in the Green Vaults, others which were formerly exhibited in the Palace, are now in the Dresden *Kunstgewerbemuseum* (Museum of Arts and Crafts) or in Moritzburg Castle.

Of the comparatively small number of objects of gold some may have originated from the Secret Deposit, but the majority were taken from the *Hofsilberkammer* (the Court's Silver Cabinet). Apparently all historically valuable goldsmiths' works in the latter were removed to the Green Vaults at that time. Yet a large number of objects of silver, mentioned in this inventory, are marked "modern". This applies in particular to basins for rinsing, ice-pails, tables, stands for candlesticks and mirrors, and also to a "silver dinner set with dull gilding which His Royal Majesty had ordered from Augsburg in 1718"; it consisted of two hundred and seventy vessels and various utensils, together with ninety-eight knives, forks and spoons, and was evidently thought to be the most valuable of the gilded dinner sets. Moreover there are several smaller dinner sets of silver, which came as it were by accident to the Green Vaults, perhaps just to fill in empty spaces, seeing that similar sets and even some of greater value were to be found in the Silver Cabinet at the same time. All this material, the historical as well as the "modern" items, was continually undergoing change through donations, removals, acquisitions, sales to pay off debts or to defray the cost of new purchases, or even through being melted down. But the main reason for all this was the tendency to modernisation which remained in force under Augustus III, 1733–1763.

Fashions probably changed as rapidly and as suddenly as nowadays, and the changes in design are less obvious only now, when seen from a distance, and seem to us only slight variants of style. At that time the role of fashion was apparently so much a matter of prestige that whole dinner sets were melted down after ten or twenty years and turned into new ones as rapidly as possible. O'Byrn's publication on the Court's Silver Cabinet in 1880 and the inventory of the Silver Room of 1723 give a good picture of these costly dealings. One may gauge the size of the Silver Cabinet at the time when some of its items were taken to the Green Vaults, from a record made in 1722 which states that besides the *Silberkämmerer* (Silver Chamberlain) Weigelt, eight *Silberdiener* (Silver Servants), and a number of other assistants and washerwomen were employed there (2).

The third and last room to be completed in 1724 was the "Hall of Preciosities". Its inventory, three hundred pages long, was signed by the King on 5th January 1725. The Hall with a surface of about 180 square metres is twice as large as either of the other two rooms. Its decoration was very ornate and probably took longer to complete than the others. According to the preface of the inventory the Hall was to be the repository of the following items: "precious drinking vessels, cabinet pieces (that is works of art showing considerable technical virtuosity, usually found in princely cabinets of curiosities), large and small time-pieces, portraits in enamel and other similar pictures, vessels of sardonyx, chalcedony, jasper, agate, cornelians; busts or half-length portraits; valuable tea-or coffee-sets; the throne of the Great Mogul; classical pendants of gold, enamelled and decorated with gems; classical chains in solid gold; big and small figures of Moors and other sculptures and curiosities made of ivory; jugs and goblets of ivory, works in filigree silver, antique jewellery chests and writing cases; jade, green jasper, vessels made of onyx or sardonyx; bowls and vessels of chalcedony; various receptacles made of agate, alabaster, cornelians, garnets, lapis lazuli, amber or serpentine; nautilus and other shells, coral-branches, coconuts, ostrich eggs; vessels and figures made of wood; statues made of metal or rock crystal; vessels of glass, not crystal, ruby glasses and multicoloured glasses."

This list explains why the hall was called the Hall of Preciosities, so as to distinguish it from the other two rooms containing silver and jewellery respectively.

The Palace in Dresden before its destruction

Here works of various kinds of art were to be assembled, the guiding principle being their precious character. They were taken from the Cabinet of Curiosities and from the Secret Deposit. The principal cabinet pieces by *Dinglinger* as well as the most precious works of rock crystal had previously been stored in the Old Treasury, but in the sixteen-thirties the latter had, in accordance with a plan described by Hainhofer, been removed to decorate the Pavilion on the Jungfernbastei. They were evidently soon brought back to the Secret Deposit, as they were handed over from there in 1668 to the Cabinet of Curiosities to be returned yet again to the Secret Deposit in 1687. Eventually they found a home in the Hall of Preciosities almost without interruption from 1725 until 1942.

The inventory of 1725 mentions certain objects taken in September 1724 from the Cabinet of Curiosities to the Hall of Preciosities, specified as figures and other curiosities of ivory, nautilus and other shells, receptacles decorated with mother of pearl, ostrich eggs and goblets made of ostrich eggs.

It may be assumed that some objects came to the Hall of Preciosities from the King's private apartments. The chains and pendants of the sixteenth and seventeenth centuries and other jewellery sets had probably been in the safekeeping of the Sovereign himself. Possibly some of the figures in ivory and of the "big and small Moors", works by contemporary Dresden modellers, had also been kept in the King's own rooms.

The equipment of the Hall of Preciosities marked the completion of the plan for a museum-like treasury. In 1723 a dog-legged staircase was built which led from a door of the Secret Deposit, probably broken into the wall in the 17th century, to a plastered courtyard adjoining the street. The new museum could also be reached from a stair-turret, by a stair which led from the turret to a room between the Hall of Preciosities and the Silver Room, which was later called the "Escutcheon Room". This was certainly the private entrance of the inhabitants of the Palace. The new entrance to the door of the Silver Room may have been planned for people interested in the Collection who did not belong to the Court or to its guests. On written application they could obtain permission from the King to visit the treasury. It was at that time that Baron von Pölnitz, an adventurer known as a scandal merchant, saw the Collection. In his *Lettres et Mémoires*, first published in 1727, he says: "The Royal treasury, generally known as the Green Vaults, is inside the Palace. It consists of three vaulted rooms, in which there are immense treasures. Wherever you look, you see nothing but gold, precious stones and diamonds. It is one of the most beautiful places in the world."[3]

Notwithstanding this enthusiastic description, the early appearance of the Green Vaults was obviously very modest compared with its eventual form, from the beginning of the seventeen-thirties to the second decade of the present century. An inventory of the Hall of Preciosities made in 1733 enumerates twice as many items as that of 1725. Evidently many new brackets had to be made to enable the recent acquisitions to be displayed. Much the same applied to the Jewellery Room. Its second inventory, signed by Augustus III on 31st October 1733, also shows a marked increase over the first one, especially in works by *Johann Melchior Dinglinger* made after 1722, and in older jewellery, which had been in the Hall of Preciosities during the twenties of the century. Accounts for the Green Vaults to be dated 1724 provide a notion of the original arrangement of the Jewellery Room; they state among other entries: "20 thaler 21 groschen to the bookbinder *Nitzschner* for lining the drawers of the jewellery cupboard with fine green glazed linen ..., 176 Thaler 2 Groschen to the joiner *Gärtner* for fitting and covering with new leather twelve shelves for jewels, further for fitting all the drawers into the jewellery cupboard and for arranging them properly."

These accounts obviously apply to the large new jewellery cupboard, mentioned in the inventory of 1722 (see above). As this cupboard was furnished with drawers, in which the jewellery sets lay on specially made boards, the accounts cannot refer to furnishings of what was later known as the Jewellery Room, because there the jewellery sets were exhibited one beside the other in open display. It may therefore be assumed that the first furnishing of the treasury, completed in 1724, was re-arranged and enriched soon afterwards, when a more extensive programme was conceived for the museum. Proof of the fact that work on the reconstruction of the Green Vaults was continued immediately after 1724, is given by the accounts made at the time of the New Year's Fair of 1726 according to which considerable sums were assigned to the stone mason *Fossati* in payment for five marble table-tops, to the sculptor *Thomae* for five stands for the same table-tops and for twelve tabourets, and to the widow of the gilder *Hoyer* for gilding the stands and the tabourets. It is expressly stated that these articles were delivered to the Green Vaults.(4)

In the spring of 1727 Augustus the Strong decided that the treasury should be enlarged. We are told of this in an (unsigned) letter to Count Wackerbart, dated in Warsaw on the 8th of March, 1727: "Your Excellency has already been informed by letter of 5th March that His Royal Majesty has decided that the vaulted rooms, where until now the meetings of the Council have been held and where the archives are stored, should be incorporated into the Green Vaults, while the apartments known as the Fürstenberg Apartment, until lately occupied by Her Highness the Princess of Weissenfels, are to be assigned to the Council." That the letter was written by Count Flemming may be deduced from a handwritten note from the King to the Count and from Wackerbart's answer to Flemming, dated 18th March, 1727.(5)

This plan to move the Council Chamber and to evacuate the archives for the sake of the Green Vaults, had evidently already been altered and enlarged by the beginning of April 1727, as is shown by a document among the records of the Green Vaults entitled "Humble and unpresuming reminder of what has to be observed in connection with the removal and alterations concerning the Silver

The large courtyard with the entrance to the Green Vaults before its destruction

Cabinet and the offices belonging to it." The document is signed "Royal Polish and Electoral Saxon Silver Cabinet", and dated 17th April 1727. This explains the royal order to the customs officer Lange, preserved among the files of the Green Vaults, item seven of which reads: "as soon as he arrives in Dresden, Lange is to make an immediate start on the builders' work in those Vaults where until now the Privy Council has been accommodated, and also in those which have been occupied by the Silver Cabinet and the kitchens. The four windows overlooking the large courtyard are to be enlarged and marble floors as well as marble doorframes are to be commissioned for the three vaults; furthermore it must be arranged that the appropriate iron doors and iron shutters for the windows should be made as soon as possible ..."

This is the beginning of the reconstruction which gave the Green Vaults its present shape. Yet no clear picture can be formed of the extent of the work started at that time, nor any concise concept of what had already been there in 1724. Only the discovery of an architect's plan in the Dresden *Institut für Denkmalpflege* (Institute for the Preservation of Monuments) explains the situation as far as the architectural problems are concerned. The plan is not dated, but as it shows the dog-legged staircase in front of the Silver Room, it cannot date further back than 1723. The sepia lines, roughly but steadily drawn, follow exactly the instructions given by the King in the spring of 1727. As the rooms of the Silver Cabinet are already included in the plan, and as the builders' work had started at once, this plan, with the lines pointing to the alterations, shows the layout of the ground floor in the west wing of the Palace as it was in April 1727.

One can see from this that the Green Vaults had until then consisted of ˜ ˜ than three rooms and that these had not yet included the room we know as the Jewellery Room; the jewels were kept in the drawers of the cupboard in the "first Green Vaults" later on known as the Escutcheon Room. Cupboards stood along the walls in this room on the bare floor, as the marble floor laid after the spring of 1727 did not reach under them; this is even today clearly discernible. No special decoration had until then been vouchsafed to this room, because – as has already been mentioned – it was merely the entrance for the inhabitants of the Palace, and there was only one window in its outer wall. It did not seem light enough to justify the sort of decoration appropriate for a museum. But as it belonged to the same suite as the Treasury, which was given sumptuous furnishings, its character had to be adapted to conform with the other rooms. Augustus the Strong arranged for this to be done at the least possible cost; his order to Lange states under item eight: "It must be ascertained how many escutcheons with the coats of arms of the provinces of Saxony are affixed to the cupboards in the Royal wardrobe and whether these could be used on the doors of the cupboards in the first Green Vaults. A plan of these cupboards, accurately showing to scale their height, width and depth is to be sent here at once."

Most of these escutcheons, obviously dating from about 1700, have been preserved; they are made in chased copper, with a wealth of openwork and gilding. They were inserted into the doors of the cupboards in the first Green Vaults, and this gave the room its name of the Escutcheon Room. Since there were not sufficient escutcheons, some additional ones were commissioned in the same style. Owing to its scanty lighting it retained its passage-like character until the present century. Only a few and not particularly prominent works of art were kept there, while the cupboards were used to store various material belonging to the Collection.

It thus appears that only two rooms of the Green Vaults had been made into show-rooms by 1727; the Silver Room and the Hall of Preciosities with the Corner Cabinet, and one must also conclude that even in these rooms the decoration was altered or at least enriched in the second building period. In fact, this period, that of the main reconstruction, only started in 1727, as becomes evident if the original maze of divisions and partitions shown on the plan of that year is compared with the clear and simple arrangement indicated by the sepia lines, drawn in with a few strokes of the pen; besides it was not till then that the Escutcheon Room, the Jewellery Room, the Enamel Room, the Bronze Room and the Ivory Room had been furnished with wall-panelling, brackets, stuccos, paintings, mirrors, glass cabinets, gilded tables, lacquer work, marble flooring and door-frames, and gilded iron doors, nor with new windows with iron lattices and shutters.

No accounts referring to this building period have yet been found, except estimates dated May 1727, for the floorings and door-frames of marble which were discovered in the archives of the Green Vaults. We do know, however, the names of some of the artists and craftsmen employed on this work, and when approximately it was completed. One of the former directors of the Collection, Theodor Graesse, wrote in the preface to his catalogue: "For the lacquer work on the walls of some of the rooms in the Royal Green Vaults done in the years 1733–1734 are named also the Court Painters *Christian Reinow*, who died 1749, and *Isaak August Wiwield*, a Dane by birth."(6) A letter written in 1734 by *Johann Joachim Kändler*, the famous modeller of the porcelain factory at Meissen, also shows that work in the Green Vaults continued at least until the beginning of the seventeen-thirties: "Having previously enjoyed the privilege of working for six years at a great many decorations for the so-called Green Vaults ..." (7) *Kändler* had become assistant to the sculptor *Thomae* in 1723; he may therefore have worked in the Green Vaults from then until 1724 and finally from 1727 until his appointment to Meissen in 1731.

But the clearest information about the length of time the reconstruction took is given in J. G. Keyssler's book "Neueste Reisen" (Most Recent Travels). He described all the rooms of the Collection in October 1730. At that time, however, there were mechanical toys and devices exhibited in the Ivory Room, and Keyssler saw the ivory pieces in the adjacent room, later on known as the Enamel Room; yet the former's colour makes it certain that right from the beginning it was planned for the exhibition of ivory. Perhaps the brackets had not yet been finished, as Keyssler reports that the mechanical devices stood on tables. All things considered, it may be assumed that the reconstruction and decoration of the Green Vaults was not completed before 1731.(8)

The mere mention of young *Kändler* and the Court Sculptor *Benjamin Thomae*, the most outstanding of *Balthasar Permoser's* assistants, shows how high was the standard achieved by the joint work of the greatest representatives of Dresden Baroque. The architects *Leplat* and *Longuelune* and the Court Jeweller *Johann Melchior Dinglinger* had submitted to the King sketches for the decoration of the Green Vaults not later than in December 1718. (9) On the accounts for furnishings in the years 1723 and 1724 we find the signatures of the Court Architects *Pöppelmann, Leplat, Longuelune* and *Knöffel*, as well as that of a prominent engineer, the Court Mechanician *Gärtner*. According to a list for payments for work in the Silver Room and the Hall of Preciosities (finished by 1724) the Court Sculptor *Thomae* was to receive 1786 Thaler, the Court Lacquerer *Martin Schnell* – one of the greatest masters in the European art of Baroque lacquer work – 507 Thaler, and *Noor*, the manager of the mirror factory in Dresden, 8487 Thaler. (10) Another artist working on the decoration of the Hall of Preciosities was the Court Sculptor *Guillaume Hulot* of Paris, who had been summoned to Berlin in 1700, but came to Dresden in 1722, probably through the intervention of his friend *Longuelune*.(11) He carved and gilded "twenty ornaments to crown the stands against the walls in the rooms of His Majesty the King of Poland."(12) This evidently refers to the heads of women with palmetto-like crowns, which form the tops of the wall-panels of the Hall of Preciosities; they are still extant.

It is at present impossible to pick out the work of individual artists, to discover early plastic work by *Kändler*, or tell whether any lacquer-paintings by *Martin Schnell* have been preserved. All the movable items of the interior decoration of the Green Vaults that still exist are, however, stored in the Dresden Institute for the Preservation of Monuments; research will become feasible after the restoration of all the rooms in the Green Vaults is completed.

The earliest description of the Green Vaults is by an unknown author; it was published in Frankfort on Main and Leipzig in 1737. At that time access to the Collection was obtained from the courtyard of the Palace and, having passed the guards, "a small apartment was reached through a long passage ... where a visitor

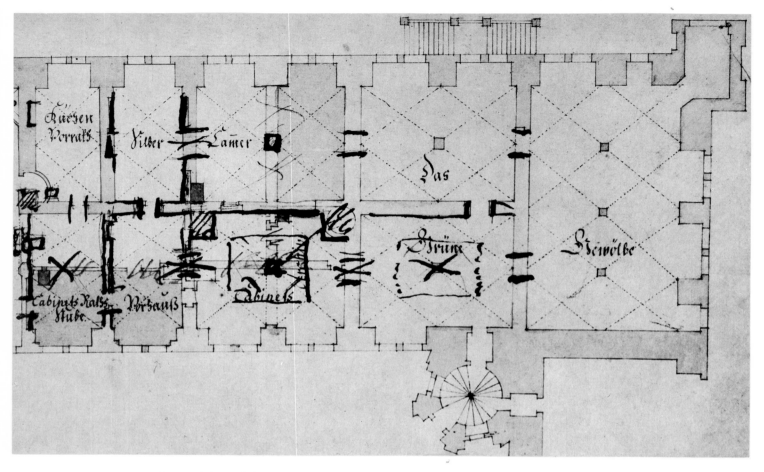

Groundplan of the west wing of the Palace with the Green Vaults in the Spring of 1727

had to deposit his sword and where a gentleman, usually a privy chamberlain, was waiting to show him round." From there the Bronze Room was entered, at that time a small room of approximately 45 square metres. The walls were covered with panelling of dark lacquered wood right up to the beginning of the vault. Large mirrors, each made of several panes, were set into the panels of the walls, brackets of comparatively modest construction were attached to the pilasters between these panels; above, the panelling ended in a shelf. Possibly the brackets were made later, as the author of 1737 asserts that in the first room "there was nothing to be seen but a few plaster statues of King Augustus II on horseback ... apart from sculptures referring to the *Metamorphoses* of Ovid, also made of plaster." Above the doors were plaster busts of the Kings of Prussia and of Poland with their wives.

This description shows that the author cannot be regarded as reliable, as the equestrian statuettes are made of bronze and the busts of gilded copper; further-

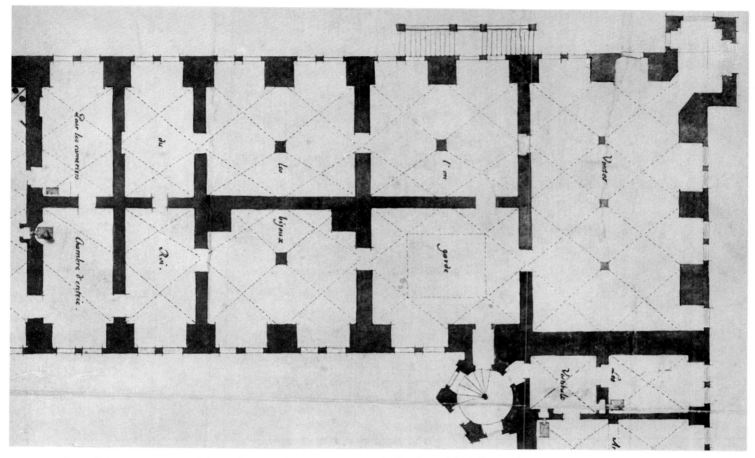

Groundplan of the west wing of the Palace with the Green Vaults in the mid-eighteenth century

more, not all of them stood above the doors. But it is interesting that the author describes the room as comparatively empty. It was probably intended to serve as a kind of ante-room. The contents of the Bronze Room were, however, increased in the course of the eighteenth century. The first inventory that we have, written in 1819, enumerates one hundred and nineteen works; since then there has not been any substantial change made in the Collection.

The next room to which the visitor was taken was the Ivory Room, at that time as small as the previous room. It too was panelled; this wooden panelling and the wooden brackets were grained. The prevailing colour in the room was a brownish violet, against which the ivory stood out exceedingly well. It seems likely that these two rooms were finished last, as their decoration differs from that of the other rooms. There was no gilded woodwork, nor apparently were the floors originally covered with marble. The author of 1737 mentioned only when he came to the description of the third room "that this, like all the following rooms, except the seventh, was decorated all round with mirror-glass panes with thin gilded supports between them; the floors were laid with polished marble." The patterns of the panelling were also relatively simple in the first two rooms. Compared with the other rooms, they seemed simple and linear, of a somewhat neo-classical style. These rooms were certainly not finished before 1730.

In the third room, later known as the Enamel Room, baroque exuberance greeted the visitor. It was twice as large as the previous room, about 90 square metres. Its vault was supported in the centre by a pillar. The panelling was in shining lacquer, deep red in colour, each of the panels was framed by pilasters covered with mirror-glass and above them were arches of shining glass in ribbon-like patterns. The capitals of the pilasters, the bases of the mirroring arches and the decorations attached to them were of elaborately carved and gilded wood. The centre of each panel was covered by a large mirror made up of several panes. On the panels between the mirrors and the shining pilasters red brackets with gilded outlines were arranged in regular rows reaching right up to the arches. In the deep embrasures of the windows shone ornamental mural paintings in red and gold. Round the mirrored central pillar and in front of the wall-panelling stood tables of richly carved and gilded wood. The floor and the frames of the doors were covered with polished Saxon marble in shades of red, grey and white.

Originally this room was used for the storing of vessels of non-gilt silver: "In this room you see masses of works of silver, built up in pyramids along the walls and the pilasters, or casually placed on tables and window-seats." As the unknown writer says, the works of silver there were mostly of an extraordinary size, "candle-sticks seven to eight feet high which can only be cleaned by using steps." None of these are preserved today. We have therefore to add in imagination to the red and gold of this room the brilliance of silver and the white and grey of the marble slabs on the floor and the dark red of the marble on the door-frames, altogether a splen-didly festive colour-scheme.

A similar scheme, but designed to show off different material, surrounded the visitor in the fourth room, the Silver Room. Here all the woodwork was lacquered in green; here too were mirrors, but the relationship between them and the wooden panels was reversed: in the Enamel Room the mirrors and the pilasters covered with mirror-glass seemed to be set on top of the wood panelling, while here the frames of the mirrors, the arches and other decorations carved in wood were fixed like broad fillets edged in gold upon the mirroring wall-panels; at the vertex of the arches as well as at their feet – precisely, that is, at the points of greatest importance from the architect's point of view – these fillets had a further decoration of patterns in gold. Rows of brackets in shining gold and green hung on the green woodwork of the arches and frames and, symmetrically arranged, also on the mirror-panels.

This room of the Green Vaults was perhaps completed in two stages; when the decorations were removed, some green panelling was discovered behind the mirrors and these had been delivered to the Green Vaults not later than in 1724. In fact the whole style of the room seems heavier and more archaic than that of the other rooms. (14)

As mentioned above, this room was reserved for works of gold or silver gilt. According to the author of 1737 the golden vessels stood "against the wall in front of a pillar". This obviously refers to the wall between the two windows, where there were ornately carved and completely gilded brackets. On the opposite wall a pillar was outlined so as to establish the symmetry so much favoured by the Baroque, and similar brackets hung in a similar order on the counterfeit pillar. In this room the warm glow of the golden and the gilded vessels stood out against the cool green of the woodwork, just as the cool shimmer of the silver vessels had done against the warm glow of the red panelling in the previous room.

The Hall of Preciosities, the fifth room, sparkled all over with gold and mirror-glass. Here the walls themselves as well as the pilasters and the arches were covered with mirror-glass; three of these pilasters had frame-like settings in gold. Special emphasis was laid upon the bases of the arches to show them in their golden glow. The brackets too were gilded, all of them richly carved, some in figurative, some in purely ornamental designs; there were hundreds of them in all shapes and sizes. They were fixed directly on to the mirrors, in which they themselves were mirrored, along with the works of art they carried, and these mirrored pictures were again multiplied in the mirrors facing them.

Approximately in 1560 the ceiling of this room was decorated in stucco by Italian masters and a new marble floor was laid. In the embrasures of the windows hung life-size full-length portraits of the Electors of Saxony; above them in the vault were ornamental mural paintings in gold, red and green. On the wall opposite the door were two gilded canopies, each raised on three steps; they were made in low-relief, but mirrors lent them an illusion of depth. Under one of them stood in the eighteenth century the principal item in the Collection, "The Princely Household at Delhi on the Birthday of the Great Mogul Aurangzeb", a work by *Johann Melchior Dinglinger*.

The Silver Room of the Green Vaults prior to 1913

The main purpose, however, for which this room was singled out was to hold the wealth of vessels made of semi-precious stone and the collection of rare coloured glasses. The large vessels of rock crystal were reflected in brilliant white in the mirrors around the room, the bowls of onyx, jasper, agate, chalcedony, cornelian, porphyry or alabaster in a great variety of colours. On the gilt tables stood the magnificent works of Limoges enamel. The report of 1737 continues: "By one of the pillars there was nothing to be seen but ostrich eggs, built up in pyramids, whole ones and half ones, all mounted in a most superbly skilled manner, as well as ostriches, enamelled and decorated with precious stones. There were also vessels

The Bronze Room of the Green Vaults prior to 1913

made of mother of pearl, nautilus or of other shells. These works were of very diverse colours, but seemed even more colourful by contrast with the lack of colour in the architecture of the room.

The splendour of the room was inevitably bewildering, and this impression was enhanced in every possible way. The mirrors made it quite a puzzle to discover where the hall began and where it ended, and it was very difficult to make an immediate estimate of the number of the precious works exhibited there. Reflections and multiplied reflections were used to produce a bewitching effect in a comprehensive work of Baroque art.

Framed by the flowing curves of heraldic cartouches, the monograms of the founder and owner of the Collection, "AR" for *Augustus Rex*, were to be seen above the doors in imposing dimensions.

Through a gilded lattice access could be gained to a small side room, the sixth room, on the ground floor of a turret; it was known as the Corner Cabinet. In the centre of the circular vault an "AR" topped by a crown was displayed on a golden and colourful ornament. Between the two windows were three narrow and two wider panels made of mirror-panes framed in gold, and on these mirrors hung the most valuable brackets of the Collection; they represented the heads of fauns and masks with different expressions, all amidst tendrils, scrollwork and ribbon-like patterns, blossoms, shells and palmettoes, forming whole garlands reaching right up to the vault. These brackets were lacquered in brown and greenish shades with consummate skill, probably by *Martin Schnell*; their main outlines were high-lighted in gold. On them stood the countless fantastic, toy-like small cabinet pieces of monstrous character, so typical of that age, figures of dwarfs, beggars and soldiers, cooks, dancers and comedians, dromedaries and craftsmen, none of them of more than a finger's length. Some were made entirely of irregular pearls or of gold and enamel, or of white or lacquered ivory; they stood on pedestals of silver, gold or ivory, amber or heliotrope, decorated with enamel paintings, rubies, diamonds and emeralds. Even today there is hardly any other collection so rich in such little figures as the Green Vaults.

The seventh room was the Escutcheon Room: "Along the side walls are cupboards, which are to contain life-size wax figures of the late King and his wife and of the present King and his wife." This plan reported by the anonymous writer of 1737 was never carried out. As mentioned above, this room with only one window was intended to be used as a passage. It was Sponsel, appointed Director of the Green Vaults in 1908, who for the first time had tables brought in and glass cabinets set into the embrasures of the window. Some larger works of comparatively little artistic value were exhibited on the tables, and in the glass cabinets a large number of small figures and time-pieces, chiefly taken from the highest brackets in the Corner Cabinet, where they had hardly been visible.

The Jewellery Room formed another climax of the whole arrangement. According to its position and its priceless contents it was to be the crown of the whole Collection. The walls were covered with mirrors; the arches set upon them and the pilasters were of glass painted on the reverse side in the technique known as églomisé painting; they were framed in gilded fretwork. The top ornament of the mirrors was provided by a heavy cornice, above which began decorative mural paintings on the walls and on the ceiling.

Glass cabinets were set into the mirror-panes which covered the walls; they served to exhibit the jewellery sets of Augustus the Strong, single pieces of jewellery, medals and costly weapons, among them even the sword of the Electors of Saxony, as well as walking sticks decorated with jewels. As we learn from the description of 1737 this jewellery lay in the glass cabinets on sloping shelves covered with black velvet. At present the jewels in the Green Vaults are no longer exhibited in this way, as there would be a danger of exaggerating their impact, but at the time of Augustus the Strong the effect of this arrangement was even further enhanced by the total appearance of the room, its marble, its gilded wood, the églomisé painting in gold, blue and red on the glass of the pilasters and arches, and by mirror upon mirror everywhere.

There had been some earlier, yet similar, forms of display in Dresden before the rearrangement of the Green Vaults at the beginning of the eighteenth century. The pavilion on the Jungfernbastei has already been mentioned; today it forms the eastern end of the Brühl Terrace; Hainhofer, the Augsburg diplomat and art-dealer, saw it in 1629, shortly before it was completed. He describes a "beautiful grotto", which he observed in the left wall of the hall on the lower floor. It consisted of "three parts"; the main lines indicating its architectural form were stressed by semi-precious stones. "This grotto", he says, "will serve as a treasury to display all the valuable vessels of crystal, jasper, topaz, agate and other foreign containers of stone with gold mounts". Here the principle was already observed of displaying works of art in surroundings, the architecture of which was especially designed to make them an integral part of the decoration. But this arrangement of the Pavilion on the Jungfernbastei was of a restricted character, as it was applied only to one wall; it may have been that of the contemporary treasuries for silver.

There was yet another arrangement of works of art for show, but it probably does not date from earlier than the beginning of the eighteenth century. In 1719 the Dresden writer Iccander wrote in his book *"Das auf dem höchsten Gipfel seiner Vollkommenheit und Glückseligkeit prangende königliche Dresden"* (The triumphant Royal Dresden, at the Height of its Perfection and Bliss): "Immediately below the tower of the Palace are two Royal state-rooms; such a wealth of precious works of gold and silver is exhibited there, bowls, goblets, pedestals etc. that anyone seeing them is bound to feel absolutely beside himself." These rooms certainly represented a preliminary form of the Green Vaults, but unfortunately we possess neither a picture nor any detailed description of them. We can merely infer from accounts of festivities such as the Dresden Miners' Festival of 1719 and from contemporary reports of the exhibition of the porcelain in the Dutch Palace that the principle observed for the arrangement of these collections was similar to that subsequently used for the Green Vaults.

Another reconstruction of the same kind as that of the treasury was started approximately between 1725 and 1730, by the turning of a room in the tower of the Palace into a Porcelain Cabinet. This was probably intended only as a temporary measure, but was actually retained for more than two hundred years because the more ambitious plan, conceived at the same time, was never completed; this was to have been the interior decoration of the Japanese Palace. The arrangement of the porcelain collection there was to resemble that of the preciosities in the Green Vaults, yet not just to occupy a suite of rooms, but rather a whole palace. Augustus the Strong died, however, shortly before the work on the interior decoration was due to start, and this whole imposing plan was left unfinished after some feeble efforts.

Thus in Dresden the Green Vaults alone represents the climax of this new method of building up museums into comprehensive works of art of interior decoration, practised since the period of Mannerism. Not only was it the last great enterprise of this sort to be completed, but the grandiose artistic quality, the integration of both – collections and furnishings – was never to be attained again. Comparable solutions as regards method and artistic quality are to be found only in Baroque libraries in Southern Germany, Austria and Bohemia.

THE GREEN VAULTS AND THE ESTABLISHMENT OF MUSEUMS IN DRESDEN IN THE EARLY EIGHTEENTH CENTURY

The foundation of the Green Vaults formed part of a far-reaching reorganisation of all the collections of the Wettinian dynasty, which took place in Dresden, the seat of their Court, in the seventeen-twenties. It may seem surprising that the ambitious Elector and King, Augustus the Strong, waited for a quarter of a century after his accession to the throne before having the huge masses of works of art in his possession sorted out into suitably representative, specialised collections. One must remember, however, that all his activities during the first decade of his reign were dictated by the catastrophic and humiliating consequences of the war he waged against Sweden. Yet he managed to build the Zwinger in the following decade. This political fantasist was not satisfied with the purchase of the crown of Poland, but aimed at becoming the founder of a large empire and a glorious dynasty. With this in view, he rebuilt the capital of his electoral ancestors into one of the most magnificent royal seats in Europe.

In all his dreams and plans he attributed special importance to the arts, as it was these which brought to the capitals splendour, fame and even historical dignity. The King was bound to realise that the manner in which his art treasures and works of scientific interest were dispersed among his castles or packed together in his Cabinet of Curiosities lagged behind the contemporary advancement of ideas and the best models of princely display. There was no building in Dresden suitable for a gallery, and as for specialised collections, only the Armory, the Anatomical Cabinet, the Cabinet of Coins and the small Porcelain Palace, recently set up and the only one which could claim to be up-to-date: Louis XIV's *Petit Trianon* had been its model. As a prince Augustus the Strong had visited on his grand tour the principal cities of France, Spain and Italy and had seen their famous art collections. He knew therefore in what way his provincial Saxon residence fell short of the ancient centres of power and of the arts. At that time power was usually manifested through the display of all branches of art, of the contemporary as well as of the historic art found in the museums.

Considering this, it is evident that the Renaissance Palace in Dresden was scarcely serviceable for such novel and ambitious claims. The King therefore gave orders, while still at war with Charles XII of Sweden, for plans to be drawn up for a fundamental reconstruction and enlargement of his residence at Dresden. In the second decade of his reign a new building of enormous dimensions was planned. It was to be attached to the Zwinger and to have long galleries, where the Royal collections were to be displayed.

Approximately in 1720, however, the King appears to have given up this project, which was as costly as it was grandiose. Instead the castles of Pillnitz, Hubertusburg and Moritzburg and the Japanese Palace were rebuilt and the work on the castle and park of Grossedlitz continued on a larger scale. But when the museums of Dresden could not be built with any great degree of wealth or luxury, but only in a spirit of compromise and restriction, the idea of a stately display of works of art in the rebuilt capital was not abandoned entirely, even though only existing buildings were used for the purpose. Yet not later than 1730 Augustus the Strong was already planning to erect a new large group of museums when the most important of his collections had hardly been put in order. It may indeed be assumed that the barely completed work was already considered inadequate and, in fact, the work of setting up the collections in more fitting buildings went on until the beginning of the Second World War.

The reorganisation of the collections of the dynasty of the Wettinians during the seventeen-twenties was an impressive achievement not only in thought and organisation, but also economically. Even today, nearly two hundred and fifty years later, the system originally devised is still firmly established. The Gallery of Paintings was founded and the top floor of the former Stables adapted to house it, while the Armory, which had occupied these rooms until then, was removed to less stately quarters. The Mathematical-Physical Salon, the collections of minerals, shells and of other objects of natural history, the residue of the Cabinet of Curiosities, the Cabinet of Engravings and the Library were housed in the Zwinger which had originally been built as an orangery. The new treasury alone was left in the Palace. The Collection of Antiquities was temporarily set up in the pavilions in the *Grosse Garten*, and the conversion of the newly built Japanese Palace into a Palace of Porcelain had just been started when Augustus the Strong died at the beginning of 1733.

By then the vast number of objects in the Cabinet of Curiosities had been sifted and distributed according to a new system. Dozens of inventories had been made of these new collections, all with descriptions and included under new categories; the system is still partly in use, providing the scholarly base for the individual collections, in marked contrast to that employed during the sixteenth and seventeenth centuries. Although some remnants of the Cabinet of Curiosities were still kept together till as late as 1832, the period of its main importance had come to an end in the twenties of the eighteenth century, and with it ended the outdated, partly rationalistic, partly speculative, partly superstitious conception of the world of the late sixteenth century. While hitherto primary importance had been ascribed to the scientific and historical character of this comprehensive collection of works of art and of mechanical devices, now preeminence was given to the arts. After the reconstruction comparative methods of research could at once be applied to the specialised and clearly arranged collections in accordance with the general trend of Enlightenment, which began to spread over Saxony at the time.

There were, however, other even more powerful forces at work to bring about the reconstruction of the collections – overdue as it was – than those occasioned by the universal historical development of the age, namely the host of officials, art-dealers, architects, builders, artists, craftsmen and scholars, as well as porters and similar workers, who were employed to strengthen and display the prestige of the new King. The museums, like the orangeries and the palaces, were shining jewels in the crown of the country, which its capital, the seat of the Wettinian dynasty, was to represent. It was a period when many new buildings and foundations of all kinds were springing up in the capitals of nearly all the states of Europe.

After the death of Augustus the Strong the Collection of the Green Vaults was increased only by a few pieces. Several snuff-boxes and some pieces of the jewellery set with brilliants show the influence of the Rococo style. Augustus III had his father's jewellery partly remodelled, evidently so as to make it more fashionable; he also acquired a few items of importance, but he did not exercise any formative influence on the Green Vaults. The reason for this is obvious. Augustus III was a passionate collector of paintings, more so than his father had been. During the thirty years of his reign a specific neo-classical Rococo was introduced into Dresden a style less distinctive than that which had prevailed in Dresden under Augustus the Strong.

It is easily understandable that a man who preferred paintings by Italian masters of the Renaissance or the Baroque, who was fond of the Rococo atmosphere and supported the neo-classical style, could not take pleasure in his father's Green Vaults, with its heavy and gorgeous style of the High-Baroque. Although hardly finished, it was outmoded. No wonder that Johann Joachim Winckelmann, then living in Dresden, despised the Collection and that Goethe took no notice of it: "Baroque" in their time denoted something done contrary to rules, which was capricious and lacking in taste, and was thought to be characteristic of despotic absolutism.

Nevertheless down to the beginning of the nineteenth century a few more pieces of jewellery were added to the treasury and others were refashioned, while in 1832 the Collection was enlarged by about five hundred items, some of them very valuable, which represented the last remnants of the Cabinet of Curiosities. Since then pieces of jewellery have been included sporadically, if it seemed that they were suitable for a collection of specifically Saxon character by virtue of their origin or their style; some came from other museums in Dresden or from the estates left by princes, while some were bought from private persons. After the seventeen-thirties acquisitions for the Collection diminished and came to an end with some single pieces of jewellery at about 1800.

The first Director of the Green Vaults, Baron von Landsberg, noted in his catalogue of 1833 that the Sovereigns no longer thought it desirable to augment the Collection. Landsberg had even to apologize to the public for the existence of the museum, and he explained: "These Collections are typical of the taste of the century in which they were made. The general level of education and knowledge of the time does not lead us to expect that a preference for true beauty would have determined the choice of the objects collected; rather, tastes were governed by a certain predilection for splendour; works requiring painstaking labour, or those of an artificial or curious nature were most highly valued; taste in fact depended not on the sublime but rather favoured refined detail. The archeologist may not be satisfied if he expects to find material for a truly antiquarian study of the basis of art, while the unprejudiced art lover will find cause for speculation as to the value of these Collections for the history of art."

Landsberg was the first to do thorough and scholarly work on this so long neglected Collection. His notes taken from files which were lost in the Second World War still find a place in the present-day catalogues. This man of refined taste, a pioneer in his own sphere, must have felt rewarded when his contemporaries gradually came over to the point of view he had held for so long. In a new catalogue, made in 1851, he was able to lay aside the apologetic tone of his earlier comment. He even went so far as to write: "The treasures of the Green Vaults form part of the vast province of art; they include many of its choicest works and everything our forbears used to admire most. They must consequently be of general interest to all educated people. Moreover they combine with their material value and antique splendour certain other charms, which are to be found hardly anywhere else, notably a splendid and appropriate setting and layout, which is probably unique of its kind. To these factors the Green Vaults owe their outstanding position among the sights of Dresden and to them must be attributed a fame which has spread throughout Europe."

These sentences hint at a change of outlook in the middle of the nineteenth century, when the bourgeois neo-Baroque period brought about a revival of interest in the Green Vaults and an understanding of the way its treasures were displayed. At the same time methods of exhibiting were steadily improved. It was a sign of the growing renown of the Collection that the number of visitors continued to increase, more was published, much of it translated into foreign languages, and more research began to be carried out on the contents of the Collection. Naturally the general growth of tourism was also a contributory factor; altogether the interest of the public and its wish to see the Collection is still increasing today, a hundred years later.

But this growing wave of public interest in the nineteenth century also created some difficulties. The Collection had been arranged as a Prince's personal Cabinet of Preciosities. Nearly all the objects stood about loose; only the jewellery was protected under sheets of glass. Yet right from the beginning people interested in seeing the Collection were permitted to do so. It was the duty of the inspector of the Collection to show single visitors or even small groups around; of course he had to be given a "testimonial" in the form of a gratuity, which was large enough to exclude people of lesser means.

In 1831 the administration of the Green Vaults was taken over by the state. From then on individuals were allowed to walk alone through the Collection. During the winter months, however, they still had to be taken in small groups, as there was no lighting. When the number of visitors increased and the control was relaxed, it was found necessary to erect breast-high iron barriers at a distance of about one yard from the walls in all the rooms; they can still be seen on photographs taken prior to 1913. Another reason for putting up the barriers may have been that after 1832 the Green Vaults became so crammed with the remaining pieces from the Cabinet of Curiosities that valuable works of art had to be put on brackets or tables within easy reach of visitors. The Collection remained in this state up to 1913.

Director von Landsberg was succeeded in 1868 by Theodor Graesse and the latter in 1882 by Julius Erbstein, all alike deserving scholars, who considerably added to the body of knowledge with regard to the Collection.

The Collection was slightly reduced in 1924, when the property of the Wettinian family was separated from that of the state and several important pieces, especially Italian vessels of rock crystal of the sixteenth century, were handed over to the former reigning family. Some of these works eventually reached the Rijksmuseum in Amsterdam after passing through private hands.

At the beginning of the twentieth century radical alterations had become necessary in the Green Vaults. The condition of the Collection contrasted unfavourably with its renown, which attracted visitors from all over the world. There was neither heating nor electric light, and in the dark and cold months of the year this was not only unsatisfactory as far as the visitors were concerned, but also led to a slow but steady deterioration of some of the items in the Collection, due to seasonal changes in the climate. Many works of art composed of heterogeneous material or of natural products cannot stand dry frost. Objects of wood or ivory may crack, bowls of semi-precious stone may break when covered with hoar-frost, and mastic, after holding different substances together for centuries, may dissolve, so that the objects it had helped to form, collapse. In a document from 1789 there are already complaints that "in the Hall of Preciosities much was damaged during the hard winter." In addition to this, a considerable number of brackets seem to have become loose or to have been damaged by woodworm.

This induced the energetic Director Jean Louis Sponsel, who held office from 1908, to have the old rooms of the Collection enlarged, restored and modernized. He was one of the leading scholars in his subject and recognized the value of the original decoration of the Green Vaults; the range of the restoration work done under his direction therefore goes to show how extensive the damage was. Electric lamps were fixed in the vaults and to the pillars and under-floor heating was installed in all the rooms. This made it necessary to replace the Baroque marble floors by new ones. Many of the original brackets had to be removed and copies put in their place. Glass cabinets were hung in the empty window embrasures of some of the rooms, matching the decoration of the various rooms in shape and colour, and small works of art which until then had stood, hardly visible, on the high brackets were exhibited in them.

The principal alteration was, however, the duplication of the surface area of the Ivory and the Bronze Rooms; the old decorations were removed and the enlarged rooms decorated in the same style. A smaller room next to the Ivory Room was also included in the exhibition and the chimney-piece made by *Neuber* was erected in it. This room was then called the Chimney-Piece Room, while the room where the chimney-piece had previously stood, the room decorated in red and used to contain works of silver, was turned into the Enamel Room. When the restoration was finished in 1913, Sponsel, however, told the Dresden Press that his original plan had been rejected. By his plan he had intended to enlarge the Collection by some further rooms in order to make possible the modern approach to art of concentrating on individual showpieces.

Owing to this reconstruction many of the works of art were moved to new positions so that the numbers of the inventories did not correspond. But this unavoidable drawback was outweighed by the improvements brought about by the renovation: the rooms were no longer crammed, the objects of paramount importance were made easily visible to visitors, in winter all the rooms were temperate and well lit so that the old system of conducted tours, dating from the time of the Cabinet of Curiosities, could now be given up. Sponsel replaced the iron barriers of the nineteenth century by new ones of more simple construction.

As a result of all this work, the Collection was at last in a situation to comply with the demands of the large number of visitors at all seasons. Yet the Green Vaults retained its special character, wherein lay its fame: it was the only complete princely cabinet of preciosities still preserved in Europe. It remained unchanged until 1942. The men in charge of it after Sponsel were Erich Haehnel and Walter Holzhausen.

The Hall of Preciosities of the Green Vaults prior to 1913

In 1942 when the war had already begun to destroy the towns from where it had started on its criminal course, the Collections of the Green Vaults were packed into crates and removed to the fortress of Königstein – where they had already been deposited during the Seven Years' War and the Wars of Liberation. The works of art were stored in the casemates, far below the ground of the old mountain fortress. At that time there was also a camp for French prisoners of war of high rank at Königstein. After the unconditional surrender on 8th May 1945 these former prisoners of war took over the command of the fortress. Several days went by before a detachment of the Red Army arrived from the battalion which had

The Hall of Preciosities of the Green Vaults prior to 1913

been specially commissioned to safeguard works of art. The Collection was then taken to Moscow and deposited in the safes of the Soviet Ministry of Finance.

The almost complete preservation of this beautiful collection, which in point of its material value is unique among all the collections in Germany, is due to several fortunate circumstances – it had all been deposited on one spot, no fighting took place there and it came quickly into the safekeeping of the specialized Soviet army group, to which were attached art historians and restorers.

That the Collection, so vulnerable because of its very composition, should have survived the chaos of the war is surprising, still more surprising is the preservation of a large proportion of the original decoration in the Green Vaults. Those who were responsible thought that the rooms were safe, situated as they were in the Palace, with its walls more than two metres thick and the windows protected by iron shutters. The costly decorations, even the tables with their marble tops, the work of court builders, were left in position. Only *Neuber's* famous chimney-piece made of porcelain slabs and semi-precious stones, was moved and put for greater safety in a narrow passage; it seemed too heavy for transport to Königstein. As it happens, this was the only major work from the Green Vaults lost in the war, as the passage was burnt out, while the Chimney-Piece Room was spared.

The Palace itself was destroyed along with the whole centre of Dresden by the air raid of 13th February 1945; the huge complex of the Palace buildings was demolished by fire, whole storeys, vaults and staircases collapsed. One group of rooms which had been considered the safest part of the Palace ever since it had first been built stood firm, namely the old Secret Deposit and its adjoining rooms, but the vault of the Jewellery Room collapsed, while the Bronze Room and the Escutcheon Room were burnt out. The lacquer painting and the gilding of the ribbon-like ornament on the iron door separating the Hall of Preciosities from the Escutcheon Room were melted and fused together by the extreme heat, and the door itself was buckled by the heat of the burning cupboards in the Escutcheon Room, but it prevented the flames from reaching the Hall of Preciosities. This saved the most magnificent of the rooms in the Green Vaults as well as the Corner Cabinet. Slight damage was done to the Silver Room, probably by flying sparks, as the iron window shutters had been blown in by the blast of high-explosive bombs. The Enamel Room and the Ivory Room were preserved, as was the Chimney-Piece Room, where there was no historical decoration. Of course even the rooms which had been saved suffered damage through blast and shock to the walls. Mirrors were broken and parts of the stucco and the gilded wall decorations fell. But all this damage could be repaired, as could that part of the Silver Room which had suffered from the fire. Only the Jewellery Room with its panes of verre églomisé, its mural paintings and its woodwork by *Thomae* and *Kändler* is irretrievably lost.

This was the gravest loss experienced by the Green Vaults as a result of the war. In the Bronze Room only simple wood-panelling and the wooden brackets made under Sponsel's direction in the style of the old decoration were destroyed, while the greater part of the Escutcheon Room was preserved, with its cupboards and its showy decorations, the big escutcheons of the Saxon provinces made in embossed copper. The special Library of the Collection, which had contained irreplaceable works, was destroyed by fire including all the card indexes and records, as well as several files concerning the foundation and the history of the Green Vaults, which had never been thoroughly examined. In addition, hundreds of accounts were lost, together with the drawings by the court jewellers of the eighteenth century. The inventories alone were saved, thanks to the care and energy of Dr. Erna von Watzdorf, one of the scholars then working in the Historical Museum, who had them removed to one of the depots outside the town shortly before Dresden was destroyed. They now form the basis for all new work on the Green Vaults.

The final salvation of those parts of the Green Vaults, which survived the catastrophe, is due to the Dresden Institute for the Preservation of Monuments. Its staff started as early as 1946 to remove the debris from the exposed building and put up a temporary roof, a very difficult undertaking in the starving town, where few houses were lucky enough to have any cover. The most important tables and tabourets, especially those with figured carving, were sent to Moritzburg Castle. The Green Vaults took charge of all other pieces of furniture in 1960. In 1962 photogrammetrical records of all the decorations were made by means of a special system devised by Gerhard Glaser, a Dresden engineer, and these were carefully taken to pieces, numbered and stored in the Institute for the Preservation of Monuments. With the aid of these records it will be possible to replace all these thousands of single pieces in their original order and former place. Meanwhile the rooms have been safeguarded by ceilings of concrete. In 1964 the restorers from the Collection of Sculptures of the Dresden State Collections started cleaning and restoring the stucco ceiling in the Hall of Preciosities, made about 1560 by masters from Upper Italy, and the somewhat later and simpler stucco ceiling in the Silver Room. The Corner Cabinet had been completely restored. These rooms of the Green Vaults were among the richest and most beautiful examples of Dresden Baroque and are the last still extant. It is planned to restore them when work on the Palace itself, the future centre of the Dresden museums, gets on the way.

The Collection of the Green Vaults and those of some of the other museums were returned to the German people by the Soviet Government in 1958. It was found possible to open an exhibition of four hundred of the most important objects in the following year. The continuous flow of visitors from many parts of the world to this comparatively small display is proof of the growing reputation of the Green Vaults. At present about four hundred thousand people visit the exhibition every year. Workrooms have meanwhile been made available in the Albertinum

The Ivory Room of the Green Vaults before its destruction

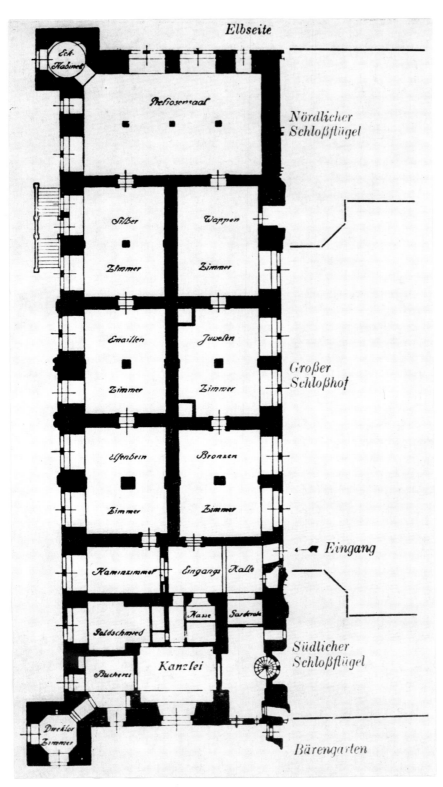

Groundplan of the Green Vaults after 1913

for those working on the Collection. Objects not included in the exhibition are put in a repository, open to specialists for study; two restorers of goldsmiths' work are in charge of it. A reference library is being built up, which at present numbers some one thousand five hundred items. Scholars and restorers have started preparatory work for an exhibition of all the treasures of the Green Vaults to be arranged in the Palace at some future date. In the Albertinum the exceptional diversity of works of art, characteristic of the Green Vaults, is shown by some of the main works: groups of works of cut stone, of silver or of silver combined with coconuts, ostrich eggs or mother of pearl; of ivory made into vessels, curiosities, or figurines, jewellery from the sixteenth century and sets of jewellery from the eighteenth century, small precious objects, and the large cabinet pieces made by the court jewellers, in particular those by *Dinglinger*. Its variety will also help to indicate the historical periods during which the Collection was formed.

THE WORKS OF ART IN THE GREEN VAULTS

The mineral resources and the history of Saxony explain the special nature of the Green Vaults. The country had been wealthy ever since silver was discovered in its mountains towards the end of the twelfth century. Other useful and valuable minerals too were found there: bismuth, cobalt, coal, tin, lead, iron-ore, together with such rare stones as agate, jasper, amethyst, smoky topaz, opal, garnet and serpentine, to enumerate only a few of them. This mining activity furthered – in what might be called a natural way – natural sciences and technology. Industries were founded early on, and specialized work of quality became traditional among the inhabitants and has survived till the present.

Works from the Middle Ages, the Renaissance, the Epoch of Mannerism, and the Baroque Dinglinger and the Eighteenth Century

Through the silver from the Erzgebirge Saxony became one of the wealthiest countries inside Germany in the late Middle Ages. An indication of this is afforded by the fourteenth and fifteenth century churches, which were erected even in small country towns in no less massive dimensions than in the Hanseatic towns of North Germany. There were of course a great many silver vessels in these churches. The sanctuary books of the early sixteenth century of Halle and Wittenberg – picture inventories as it were of the holy relics owned by the churches – give some idea of the fabulous treasures held by the main churches of Central Germany. Less is known about the goldsmiths' work owned by the princes. Sumptuous jewellery is reproduced in the portraits of Lucas Cranach the Elder, Court Painter in Saxony, who had made the wooden sanctuary book for Wittenberg, but we do not know anything about the silver in the possession of the Wettinian princes kept either for use or for show. The only information that is available from a few inventories confirms that the silver cabinets in the splendid castles of the Dukes of Saxony contained an outstanding wealth of silver at that time, hardly any of which has been preserved. (15)

After the Reformation the sacred relics gradually fell into disrepute, their costly containers of precious metal were melted down and fragments of them used to make secular vessels. Evidence of the mediaeval goldsmiths' art was thereby destroyed in such parts of Germany as formed the nucleus of the spread of the reformed faith. While this is obvious enough, we can find no explanation for the disappearance of the secular vessels and jewellery of the Saxon Dukes. One can only surmise that these treasures too were destroyed during the Renaissance. There are several showy goblets in the Green Vaults of a typically neo-Gothic shape dating from the early seventeenth century, but it is improbable that any of the

The Jewellery Room of the Green Vaults before its destruction

The Enamel Room of the Green Vaults before its destruction

Gothic pieces which they resemble were still in existence when they were made. No goblets from the late Middle Ages have been preserved together with those of the seventeenth century. We may assume that it was the iconoclasm in the epoch of the Reformation and the general determination during the Saxon Renaissance to make a fresh start with everything, which were responsible for the fact that the richest treasury of central Europe is poor in works of mediaeval art.

The choice of what was preserved from that period is most revealing: vessels of rock crystal, jasper, agate, serpentine, Syrian glass and, in addition, eight gryphon claws. Thus the Green Vaults possesses more of these ancient horn drinking vessels than any other collection. Although none of them can be identified with those mentioned in the inventories of the fifteenth century, it seems likely that some of them had belonged to the Saxon dynasty ever since that time. In view of the fact that by the middle of the sixteenth century much more important treasures had already been melted down, their preservation can hardly be due to the grandsons' regard for what had belonged to their forefathers, more probably it may be attributed to the small amount of silver in the mounts which did not make their destruction seem worthwhile. The same may have applied to the vessels of semi-precious stone. Some objects which were meant for secular use from the outset, or where the original sacred use was not clearly recognisable, have survived, like the goblet of Queen Edwiga of Poland or the small vessel of similar shape of rock crystal of the fourteenth century, which is probably French. In the case of these vessels the stone bodies were valuable enough to be preserved, even after the original mount had been removed and their first purpose had become obscure. There are in the Collection several goblets of rock crystal of the Middle Ages set in Renaissance or Baroque mounts, and two goblets of jasper of the fifteenth century which show vestiges of an original mount in gold. (16) These objects were comparatively inconspicuous and were kept in a cupboard full of fragments, known as the "supply store", from which the court jewellers were probably again and again given single items to make new works of art of them. The discovery of the vestiges of the gold settings confirms the surmise that the preservation of these gryphon claws and vessels of semi-precious stone was due to the inferior quality of their mounts.

The Green Vaults also possesses some mediaeval works in enamel from Limoges and several plaques of ivory, mainly diptychs or parts of them, carved in Paris or Cologne in the fourteenth and fifteenth centuries; some of them came to the Green Vaults from the Cabinet of Curiosities. The principal item, a Byzantine plaque of the tenth century, showing the apostles John and Paul, was only added to the Collection in 1855, when it was acquired from the chapel of the Taschenberg Palace in Dresden.

This survey of the collection of mediaeval works in the Green Vaults shows that the majority of them were not of Saxon origin. Most of the vessels of semi-precious stone were Venetian or French, and some excellent mounts of gryphon claws came from Southern Germany. Hardly anything therefore can be learned from the Green Vaults about mediaeval goldsmiths' work in Saxony.

From the first half of the sixteenth century there are again only a few solitary works in the Collection. The Albertinian branch of the Wettinians was not at that epoch invested with the Electoral dignity, and, though wealthy, was of secondary rank. In 1547 after the battle of Mühlberg Duke Maurice of Saxony acquired the title and rights of an Elector as well as some important portions of territory from the Ernestinian branch. The town and the Palace of Dresden were only then developed as a place of consequence, a strongly fortified princely seat. The yield of silver from the Erzgebirge increased at that time by leaps and bounds. In the mining district of Freiberg output increased five-fold between 1524 and 1550, reaching its maximum value of 33,650 Mark in 1572. (17) In addition there were the riches of the secularised monasteries, which fell to the ruler and to the towns, and the fact that tribute was no longer sent to Rome from Saxony. The outcome of all this is still visible today. In the second half of the sixteenth century monumental town halls were erected in the market-places of the towns, and the princes built more than ten mighty castles, most of them with four wings, at places of strategic and economic importance in their territory.

As a consequence of this the Green Vaults contains more works of art from the second half of the sixteenth century, while those of the first half are not so numerous and stand in a class of their own. One of the most beautiful items is a basin for rose-water with a jug belonging to it, dating probably from the thirties of the sixteenth century. The basin is covered with small plates of mother of pearl; the core of the jug is of copper; its shape suggests an oriental origin. The German goldsmith who had the job of making a mount for this precious and exotic piece worked with great care. He made a neck of silver for the jug, using it to cover the original long conical neck of copper; he also made a new spout and simply fitted it over the coarse one of the oriental craftsman. He joined these parts to each other and to a new silver stand by means of straps and finally secured it all with mastic. He was equally careful in making the mount for the basin. The silver-gilt hoops and the pedestal are held together by mastic and by pegs driven into the wooden core of the basin. When one lifts the basin from the pedestal, one sees that its base is covered with bright red lacquer, as is often the case in similar oriental works of mother of pearl. Such things were very much sought after as cabinet pieces in the sixteenth century; many of them may have come via Venice and Nuremberg to the Green Vaults, which owns several later specimens of that kind with work added to them by Nuremberg masters; the latter probably also made the mounts for the rose-water basin and the jug. Their decoration, which can be traced back to sketches by *Peter Flötner*, shows accomplished craftsmanship both in the cast and in

Corner-decoration of a mirror-covered pillar from the Hall of Preciosities
by Johann Joachim Kändler (?), 1724

The Exhibition of the Green Vaults in the Albertinum

the chased parts; they are certainly the work of one of the great masters of German goldsmiths' art in this centre.

The use of acanthus-leaves with large lobes in the decoration of the basin and the jug seems to point to a similarity with a large pilgrim's flask nearly 81 cm. high; this too does not show any master's mark; it is one of the most impressive objects in the Collection. Closer comparison shows, however, that the similarity is due mainly to the more or less contemporary origin of the two pieces. The individual motifs in the decoration of the pilgrim's flask are not as homogeneous as those on the basin and the jug, but are a mixture of Italian and South-German elements, and the chasing too is less delicate than that of the works which were probably made in Nuremberg. Smaller flasks of this kind are not rare, but the size is unusual. Sponsel speaks of a comparable flask at Vienna, which is supposed to have been found in Croatia. There is, however, yet another large flask in silver which is somewhat similar in the Museum of Arts and Crafts at Budapest, which is said to have come from the estate of the Hungarian King Matthias Corvinus (1458–1490). All this considered, it is obvious that the place of origin of this remarkable work of art must have been one of the art centres of Austria-Hungary. The two scenes on the round central panels have not yet been elucidated; they represent respectively five commanders besieging a town and a peasant on horseback with a prisoner of war. The form of the buildings and the landscape shown on the panels suggests that the goldsmith was acquainted with works of the Danubian School.

There are in the Green Vaults two works signed by a renowned artist of that School, the woodcarver *Peter Dell* from Würzburg: two panels of limewood, one with scenes of the "Crucifixion", dated 1528, and the other with scenes of the "Resurrection of Christ in Limbo", dated 1529. Both works were made for Duke George the Bearded (der Bärtige) of Saxony, while the master was staying in Saxony. The reliefs reveal a truly artistic mastery of form in spite of the freakish wealth of figures and their complicated symbolism, which numerous inscriptions, each inside a painted frame, endeavour to explain. The reliefs were already highly valued in the sixteenth century and are mentioned as objects of special interest among the treasures of the Wettinians in the first inventory of the Cabinet of Curiosities in 1587.

In 1548, one year after Duke Maurice of Saxony had become Elector, the construction of a new west wing of the Dresden Palace was started, a monumental building befitting the new dignity of the Albertinian branch of the dynasty. It was not completed, however, until 1554, one year after Duke Maurice's death in the battle of Sievershausen. The new ruler, Elector Augustus, was a man of advanced views, much interested in science, and he founded the Dresden Cabinet of Curiosities in 1560. It was one of the earliest museums of Europe and was housed on the top floor of the new wing of the Palace.

Notwithstanding the early date of its foundation, the Cabinet of Curiosities of Elector Augustus did not as a collection of works of art occupy a prominent place in the history of museums. In fact, it contributed little to the development of the new conception of art which had started to spread north of the Alps towards the late fifteenth century. The progressive outlook of the Elector did not manifest itself in the fine arts or in philosophy, and his humanistic knowledge probably did not exceed that of the average man of his rank. He was not a collector of works of art like Cardinal Granvelle or Emperor Rudolph II, but was interested in the applied sciences. His Cabinet of Curiosities was for the most part a collection of new and costly instruments and scientific apparatus, of books pertaining to medicine, agriculture and surveying and also to ballistics, astronomy and astrology, to mathematics and the calculation of time, to geography, architecture and mineralogy. He was of course interested in all sorts of rare natural products and curiosities and these formed part of his collection, in any case in so far as they seemed suitable for the advancement of knowledge, for study or as the subjects for explanation in scientific terms. The Collection was not arranged according to any philosophical system: subject simply followed upon subject, and it obviously gave rise to no problem when the individual groups overlapped. Works of art were only interspersed here and there. A few of those more generally known may be mentioned: there were some small landscapes by *Hans Bol*, now in the Gallery of Paintings, and bronze figurines by *Giovanni da Bologna*, the majority of which were presents from the Grand Duke of Florence. There were several works of rock crystal, presents from the Duke of Savoy, most of which were stored in the Secret Deposit; only the more remarkable ones were put into the Cabinet of Curiosities: there was a large, almost perfect sphere and a standing mirror, probably from the workshop of the brothers *Saracchi* in Milan, both of which are still in the Collection. Moreover at that time there were already in the Cabinet of Curiosities a considerable number of turned works of ivory, goblets and curiosities, of which several hundreds are still there. These objects are typical of the artistic taste prevalent at the Saxon Court at that time: they bear witness to intricate speculations about form, and were constructed with technical instruments as complicated as they were new; these included specially made drills, turner's paring knives and eccentrically working lathes. Connoisseurs were bound to be fascinated by the subtle calculations that these objects entailed, as well as by the splendid mastery of technique, the unheard-of innovations of form, and the triumphs achieved over all difficulties, even those of statics.

Another section of the Collection consisted of works of cut stone, dating from the reign of Elector Augustus. There are three main groups of these: the most important consists of vessels of semi-precious stone, particularly of rock crystal with settings from Milan, most of them from the workshop of the brothers *Saracchi*. Besides these are a number of bowls of various kinds of jasper and of chalcedony of various colours, also of Italian origin; like the rock crystal vessels from Milan with their decoration of figured and abstract designs, they too testify to the wonderful technique of polishing practised in the workshops of Northern Italy. They are mostly smooth and plain and their mounts are simple hoops of gold and enamel which seem strictly functional. The chief asset of these vessels is the beauty of the polished stone. This is sometimes ground so thin as to become translucent in parts of the surface so creating a colourful interplay with the thicker and denser parts and their velvety shimmer.

The second group is smaller. It consists of simpler goblets of rock crystal, either not decorated at all or merely cut with a polygonal pattern; probably most of them were made in Freiburg im Breisgau.

The third group comprises works of Saxon serpentine. This stone had been mined since the fifteenth century at the edge of the Erzgebirge near the village of Zöblitz, not far from Dresden. Elector Augustus, a good economist, supported this industry, probably because it seemed useful for the increase of exports, which he was anxious to expand, almost in the manner of later developed mercantilism. The Green Vaults owns numerous vessels of serpentine, all with a characteristic solid form. Several of them are rather bulbous; they were used for storage, as the stone kept the contents cool. The Dresden goldsmith *Urban Schneeweiss* made ribbon-like settings for them, which he decorated with etchings in Moresque designs. The coats of arms of Saxony and of Denmark are engraved on the gilt lids: the Elector's wife was a Danish princess. These vessels probably date from the fifteen-seventies. Their shape is not as conventional as that of the silver-gilt goblets, and this departure from courtly elegance to weighty solidity represents a special trait of the Renaissance in Saxony.

Urban Schneeweiss, 1536–1600, is one of the earliest goldsmiths from Dresden known to us by name. He and *Valentin Geitner*, who became a master in 1580, produced some works of very fine quality in the Collection. While nothing definite is known of any earlier goldsmiths from Dresden or of any work by them, the Collection contains several works by Nuremberg masters of the second half of the sixteenth century, in particular by *Wenzel Jamnitzer* and those grouped around him.

Jamnitzer, who was born in Vienna in 1508 and died at Nuremberg in 1585, was one of the outstanding goldsmiths of the Renaissance. The Green Vaults owns a small writing case by him with the sculpture of a sitting figure on the lid; it is reminiscent of Etruscan sarcophagi. The composition is severe, for strictly vertical and horizontal lines prevail. But ribbon-like ornaments stress the case's character of a miniature work of architecture. There is a frieze of triglyphs, acanthus-leaves and bead-mouldings of classical design, which is in keeping with the meaning of the silver figure crowning the case, an allegory of philosophy. The figure holds a gilt plaque with Latin verses in praise of science; on the reverse side of the plaque there is engraved a table of mathematical figures, the inscription "tabula Pythagora" and the date 1562. Only the mound on which the figure sits has no connection with classical art for it is composed mainly of sand, pebbles and crystals. A vase of crystal stands there with a twig of silver, as well as a silver-gilt casket and a tiny frog and a beetle, cast in silver from nature. The twig and the dead animals were first embedded in clay, this was baked in the oven, during which process the animals dissolved into powder and the vacuum thus formed was then filled with molten silver. The mound, the twig, the beetle and the frog were natural products converted into works of art by technical means.

In the epoch of Mannerism transformations of this kind were made from very different materials. In the Green Vaults in particular such hybrid objects were not rare, especially works with relation to minerals, as Saxony held a leading position in the science of mining in Europe. Products of nature, pretending to be works of art, and works of art, copying products of nature, were in great demand for all cabinets of curiosities in the Mannerism era. Both science and contemplative philosophy at that period considered these objects as worthy of observation and consideration. Owing therefore to its connection with natural science as well as to its ornament in imitation of classical designs, the writing case by *Jamnitzer* is an outstanding example of German art of the time.

If a secret lock is opened, one of the narrow ends of the case, that nearest to the feet of the figure, can be lifted. Inside are several little drawers of ebony, lined with satin, to hold the writing materials, a silver inkpot and a box for blotting sand. The sides of the drawers are fitted with very thin plates of silver gilt with ornaments made of ribbons of pressed silver; the negative parts of the design are lacquered in colour. A frieze of triglyphs, running round below the cornice of the writing case on the outside, was a technical innovation in the history of goldsmiths' work. The frieze was cast in a mould, made by the yard and sold to other masters, a technique which soon became popular. Cast single parts, purchased and used by various masters in different towns, are to be found on many a work of silver dating from the end of the sixteenth or the early seventeenth century. This was the beginning of an industrial method of production, which by the eighteenth century was to bring about a complete change in the technical structure of that branch of art.

There are in the Green Vaults two works by *Jamnitzer's* sons *Abraham* and

Barthel. The former made a "Daphne" with coral branches cast from a model by *Wenzel Jamnitzer*. *Barthel Jamnitzer* was responsible for only one not very impressive goblet made of a nautilus. Finally there is a work in the Collection by the other great artist of the family, *Wenzel's* grandson *Christoph Jamnitzer*. It is a jug; according to the first inventory of the Silver Room a basin once belonged with it, but this is now missing. It may have been sold or melted down in the eighteenth century, as was the practice when new table-ware in silver was wanted. The jug with its dragon-like handle and spout and its body devised with almost exaggerated refinement, nearly hidden by decorations, is a splendid example of the fantastic art of late Mannerism in Germany, of which *Christoph Jamnitzer* is one of the principal creative exponents.

One of the most gifted disciples of *Wenzel Jamnitzer*, *Nicolaus Schmidt* of Nuremberg, created seven pieces in the Green Vaults, and these constitute the major part of his still extant work. Among them is one of the chief items of the Collection, outstanding as evidence of the art of the German goldsmiths of the late Renaissance. It is a large jewellery chest, which was given as a Christmas present by Elector Christian I to his wife and added to the Cabinet of Curiosities in 1589. A drawing in Leningrad shows that its structure can be traced back to a sketch by *Wenzel Jamnitzer* and quite a number of the cast parts of it obviously came from the *Jamnitzer* workshop, for instance the frieze of triglyphs. Originally the chest was crowned by a clock with a turning dial; it seems to have been shaped like a globe. A female figure, lying on an artificial block of ore, indicated the hours with a staff. The structure and the decoration of this work are highly ornate. Between all the niches made of glass with black interlining stand columns and relief figures of kings, and in the niches themselves sculptured figures representing the virtues. Parts of the decoration in silver alternate with gilt ones. The whole chest is lined with pieces of velvet or silk in various colours, and plates of mother of pearl; pearls and precious stones form shining points in the colourful outside structure. No doubt many of the parts in silver were originally lacquered, but as almost four hundred years have gone by since the chest was made, much of the colouring has faded as a result of exposure to the light and through repeated cleaning. It is all the more surprising to find in the interior the original colours unharmed, as if the chest had only left the master's workshop a few days ago. On the gleaming base of yellow, red, blue and white silk and between golden braids, are fleurons with grotesques, and the figures of Charity, Justice and the Ascension of Christ all in silver relief and painted with translucent lacquer in sensitive, cool and subdued shades. The colours are further toned down and cooled by the white shimmer of the underlying silver, which increases the effect and harmonizes the various shades. This produces an interplay of colours typical of the refinement which dominated the Courts of Europe in that century influenced by Spanish fashion, so severe, formal, abstract and subtle.

Finally mention must be made of one more significant and splendid work by a Nuremberg goldsmith of that time, the Calvary by *Elias Lencker*, which came to the Green Vaults from the Cabinet of Curiosities; it dates from 1577. The pedestal is made of ebony with two drawers in it; the statuettes in the niches and the reliefs are of silver gilt and depict scenes from the Passion of Christ. The mountain is made of a grotesque mixture of nautilus shells, irregular pearls and some single turquoises, emeralds and garnets. Within the mountain is a cave, in it stands a heron cast in silver; on the mountain are twigs, frogs, beetles, lizards and a grasshopper, cast in silver from nature. Christ's loincloth is of translucent red lacquer. In this devotional image for domestic use there are mingled the piety and the love of splendour of the fashionable world, art and nature, the playful and the earnest, the warm glow of the silver gilt and the cool shimmer of the mountain of pearls.

The mode of life at the Saxon Court was determined at the time chiefly by Anna, the Elector's wife, one of the most fashionable ladies of the Empire. What is left of her jewellery shows her to have been a keen lover of luxurious goldsmiths' work of first-rate craftsmanship. Looking at her portraits, her slim figure, dressed and adorned strictly in accordance with the rules of international fashion as observed at the Courts, one can well imagine that she was the owner of *Lencker's* devotional image.

Some of the most beautiful works of Renaissance jewellery in the Collection once belonged to her, as is shown by the letter "A" – sometimes an interlaced "AA" for Augustus-Anna – with which they are marked at the centre. There are several chains of gold and enamel to be worn as girdles. One of them, dating from the mid-sixteenth century, is formed entirely of gold and beads of lapis lazuli. Others are made in elaborate scrollwork by first-class masters. Then there are two pendants with the single and with the double interlaced "AA", these letters always surrounded by table-cut diamonds. The pendant with the double "A" forms a set with a smaller piece, the centre of which consists of a rosette of rubies and emeralds. They may have come from the same workshop in about 1560. The decoration on both of them is highly concentrated and any parts of their surfaces where there are no gems are completely covered with scrollwork, fruits, heads and figures, motifs of *Jamnitzer*, all in solid high-relief of coarse shape. They may have been made by a Saxon goldsmith. In spite of a general similarity of shape, the pendant with the single "A", which is flanked by two genii holding a laurel wreath, differs from them through the more subtle treatment of details and the refinement of the lines. It is more closely related to the *Fontainebleau* school and may well have been the work of a French artist. The pendant with St. George fighting the dragon, probably dating from the third quarter of the sixteenth century, may also have belonged to Elector Augustus and his wife. It is an outstanding piece among the wealth of such jewellery in the Green Vaults, a miniature sculpture of amazing perfection. The muscles of the horse stand out clearly, indicating the tension of the fight. The knight leans forward in a dramatic movement and pierces with his lance the throat of the dragon, simultaneously wounding its body, where the blood shows as a large convex ruby. Because of the strength of the expressions and the wonderful delicacy of workmanship in every part, one may assume that this, one of the very best works of its kind, was made in Southern Germany.

The description of some of the principal works of various kinds has already taken us to the end of the sixteenth and the beginning of the seventeenth century, that is considerably further than the life-time of Augustus, the founder of the Cabinet of Curiosities. He died in 1586; in 1587 the first inventory was made of the Cabinet of Curiosities, and in 1588 that of the Secret Deposit. These documents do not merely provide information about the preciosities and other show-pieces in the possession of the Elector and his family at that period, but also allow us to draw some conclusions with regard to the owner's activity as a collector, his ideas about art and even his general outlook. The second inventory of the Cabinet of Curiosities, dated 1610, shows that both Christian I (1586–1591), and Christian II (1601 to 1611), the son and grandson of the founder, changed the Collection's original trend: they acquired, together with mechanical devices and objects of interest to natural science, considerably more curiosities and preciosities. The influx to the Court of Saxony of first-rate works by goldsmiths, objects of cut stone or turned ivory and of jewellery, which can be traced back to the mid-sixteenth century, increased steadily until the beginning of the Thirty Years' War. Thus there are still over eighty goblets and curiosities of ivory in the Green Vaults signed by the Dresden Court Turners *Egidius Lobenigk* and *Georg Wecker* with dates ranging from the fifteen-eighties to 1620. In addition the Collection contains some works by *Georg Friedel*, a Court Turner from the Palatinate of the Rhine and finally by *Jacob Zeller*, who was the greatest artist among these masters. He made his principal work in Dresden in 1620, a large frigate of ivory: because of its unique technical perfection and its costliness, it is a true curiosity. The billowing ivory sails, with the coat of arms cut into them in relief, are as thin as parchment, and all the guns and the rigging are of gold. Most amazing, however, is the plastic group which forms the pedestal: Neptune in his shell-shaped chariot drawn by sea-horses and accompanied by tritons. This carved work shows the Court Turner as a talented sculptor, influenced by the Mannerism prevailing in Prague and proving himself equal to the masters of his native Southern Germany.

The collection of works of silver was enriched in 1592 by an important work by a goldsmith from Lüneburg, *Luleff Meier*. It is an ornate mirror, in the shape of an epitaph, and evidently influenced by Dutch models. It is difficult to understand in detail the allegories displayed all over the mirror; they represent a prophecy based on the Old Testament: the Holy Roman Empire becoming for ever the peaceful Fourth Power.

The circle of those producing goldsmiths' work widened towards the end of the sixteenth century. Names from Augsburg were now to be found alongside those of the renowned Nuremberg masters, and at the same time Saxon masters too were producing works, which could hold their own in the eyes of the Court and in comparison with those of South-German masters. Among the goldsmiths from Dresden *Valentin Geitner* and *Georg Mond* are represented by some excellent works. From Leipzig a number of works by *Elias Geyer* came to the Cabinet of Curiosities and to the Silver Cabinet and eventually reached the Green Vaults. The pieces by this master make it seem likely that he had worked as a journeyman in Nuremberg, as they are of a considerably higher artistic standard than those of his contemporaries of the Leipzig guild. This ensured them a prominent place in the Cabinet of Curiosities and among the Elector's treasures of silver, a place they still deserve to occupy even today. His drinking vessels shaped as gryphons, basilisks, tritons, sea-horses or ostriches set in silver and nautilus shells or in ostrich eggs are among the most fantastic in the whole Collection, while the jug with the mother of pearl inlay and the jade tankard are among the objects of greatest refinement dating from the early seventeenth century. A basin by *Elias Geyer*, decorated with hunting scenes, is one of the finest examples of the German silversmiths' art of the early Baroque period. Here one finds combined a complete mastery both of plastic form and of perspective, from the large sculptured circular parts in the foreground to the engraving showing what is happening in the distance. None of the Nuremberg masters could have chiselled the details more delicately. In cut stone it was mainly works from Prague that came to Dresden, as there were good relations between the Saxon Electors and the Imperial Court at that time.

Both Christian I and Christian II were the easy-going heirs of a prominent man and lived on the riches that Elector Augustus, clever economist that he was, had accumulated. Both of them loved splendour. Although they were evidently not overmuch interested in art, several curiosities of the most subtle refinement increased the Collection during their reigns, works combining technical and artistic achievements in an astounding manner. The best known item of this kind is a cherry stone, set in gold as a pendant, into which one hundred and eighty heads have been cut with the finest drills and knives. Some of the heads can be quite clearly distinguished, for instance there are skulls, and heads of Turks and of burghers. The stone was given to Christian I in 1589 by Christoph von Loss auf Pillnitz.

Saxony was not only the country where German Protestantism originated, but also at that time the most powerful principality in the Protestant part of the Empire. Considering this, one may well compare the manner in which the Princes of Saxony furthered their Collection, mainly looking for spectacular and curious pieces, with the high level of art appreciation which had by now reached other Courts north of the Alps, for example Imperial Prague and Munich. One cannot avoid the impression that there was a tendency towards a sort of provincialism, a trend which even increased under Elector John George I (1611–1656).

Under this Prince Saxony lost its position as the leading Protestant power. During the Thirty Years' War he sided alternately with the Emperor and with Gustavus Adolphus of Sweden, with the result that his country was cruelly devastated by the supporters of both parties, its mining and textile industries badly damaged and the population decimated. But there may well be some truth in Philipp Hainhofer's statement of 1629 that "several millions of gold" were hidden in the treasury vaults of Dresden, for it is obvious that none of the precious works owned by the Elector were converted into money during the Thirty Years' War, as was usually done in those days when emergencies demanded. On the contrary: in 1635 John George I gave orders for a goblet composed of gold coins weighing over 1390 gramm to be made for each of his four sons by the Dresden goldsmith *Abraham Schwedler*. The goblets are well shaped and of creditable craftsmanship, but their standard as works of art is inferior to the value of the material.

The Cabinet of Curiosities was enriched by several important pieces in spite of the terrible times. At first, up to the sixteen-twenties, the acquisition of preciosities and jewellery continued in the same way and to the same extent as under John George's two predecessors. In 1624 works of agate and jasper were bought for 2,229 gulden; in 1622 paintings, books and statuettes were added to the Collection from the estate of the architect and sculptor *Giovanni Maria Nosseni*. But the most valuable addition came in 1623 from the estate of Sophia, the widow of Christian I: her private cabinet of curiosities, containing valuable furniture, time-pieces, small chests, paintings, ornate vessels and jewellery, altogether filling four rooms. This collection includes several major works, for instance *Wenzel Jamnitzer's* writing case and the large chest for jewellery made of silver and ebony by the Dresden master *Hans Kellerthaler*.

It may be assumed that even during the Thirty Years' War some works by contemporary Dresden masters, such as *Sebastian Dattler*, *Daniel Kellerthaler* and *Martin Borisch*, were acquired by the Elector; these works are now in the Green Vaults. They show that by the first half of the seventeenth century the goldsmiths of Dresden had become familiar with the international style of High Baroque and had attained a remarkably high artistic level. Yet the silversmiths' works in Augsburg Baroque contained in the Collection of the Elector, the two magnificent supporting figures for globes, are in every way superior. In 1629 Philipp Hainhofer had already described them as prominent items in the Cabinet of Curiosities.

After the middle of the century, during the reign of John George II (1656–1680), a significant change of policy took place in the running of the Dresden Collections. The architect *Wolf Kaspar von Klengel*, advisor to the Elector in matters of art, evidently succeeded in interesting his master in the fine arts, a sphere which had more or less been despised until then. *Klengel* was sent to Italy to purchase works of art, and returned with several valuable paintings of the sixteenth and seventeenth centuries and some sculptures by *Giovanni da Bologna* and *Melchior Barthel*: the latter was eventually appointed Court Sculptor in Dresden. Some excellent ivory sculptures of his are in the Green Vaults. Nevertheless the course which Christian I had so vigorously pursued as a collector, the acquisition of precious vessels, was also followed up. Thus in 1668 a whole collection of vessels made of rock crystal and smoky topaz was bought for twenty thousand Thaler. In the previous year an iron group of St. George by *Gottfried Leygebe* reached Dresden as a present from the Elector of Brandenburg.

This sculpture was accompanied by a report on its amazing origin, which was confirmed by Sandrart, who wrote about it in his "Teutsche Academie" of 1679. There he reported that the master had sculptured the group by carving it out with a hammer and a graving tool from a block of iron weighing sixty-seven pounds. It was not discovered until 1962 that this report was false. *Leygebe* riveted together the cast-iron parts of the group and, while chiselling, granulated the rivets and the points where the pieces had been put together, so that the joints cannot be seen even with a magnifying glass. This was discovered only by chance. From one or two remarks in his letters we must conclude that the master himself was the perpetrator of the fraud, which certainly raised the price of the group. There are two similar works by him, one at Copenhagen and one at Berlin.

It is obvious that towards the end of the seventeenth century such technical marvels were still highly valued objects, worthy of inclusion in the cabinets of curiosities of the great princely families, especially at the Protestant Courts of North-Eastern Germany. It is to this concept of art, based as it was on technical achievements, that we owe *Johann Melchior Dinglinger's* monumental works of jewellery, generally speaking the last of the curiosities.

There are in the Green Vaults only a few objects to bear witness to the artistic skill of the Dresden goldsmiths after the Thirty Years' War, some works of good quality but without any real significance for the history of art. One outstanding show-piece of this epoch is the Miner's Outfit made in 1678 by *Samuel Klemm*, a goldsmith in Freiberg in Saxony; it is a complete outfit to be worn by John George II in the Electoral procession during the Dresden mining festival; this was to demonstrate the great importance of mining to Saxony. Only semi-precious stones of Saxon origin were used as decoration: smoky topaz, rock crystal, opals, amethysts and garnets. All the work in silver, whether cast, chiselled, engraved or embossed, is excellent. The enamelled parts, also made by *Klemm*, show inscriptions and scenes connected with mining. The whole arrangement is akin to popular art; it is naive, colourful and variegated with a somewhat heavy Baroque profusion. Although the workmanship is good and the outfit is unique of its kind, yet it is provincial compared with the contemporary achievements at the Court of Louis XIV.

The development of art in Dresden during the second half of the seventeenth century appears to be full of contradictions. The pre-war standard had not yet been reattained, but a tendency towards a more modern concept of art began to show in the collectors' activities, in line with the more progressive Courts of Europe. Towards the end of John George's II reign the *Grosse Garten* was laid out and a palace built in it – the first undertaking of this kind in Germany since the disastrous war. A new era began in several artistic fields in the cultural life of the Court, thus the Court's orchestra was reorganised and Heinrich Schütz (1585–1672), a precursor of Bach with regard to choral music, was made its conductor.

John George III (1680–1691) continued to follow this new trend, but without much result. Some paintings of value were bought, but the Cabinet of Curiosities acquired no additions of consequence specifically through him.

Yet the new trends in the pursuit of art at the Court and the steady recovery of the country were responsible for bringing two men to Dresden, whose influence was to become decisive in promoting the glorious heyday of the arts in that city: the Bavarian sculptor *Balthasar Permoser*, and *Mattheus Daniel Pöppelmann*, an architect from Westphalia. When John George IV had come to the throne in 1691, an unknown journeyman came to Dresden from Swabia, the goldsmith *Johann Melchior Dinglinger*, thus bringing together there the three illustrious masters of the Dresden Baroque, even before Duke Frederic Augustus of Saxony had become Elector through the death of his brother John George IV.

Frederic Augustus I, in 1694 Elector of Saxony and from 1697 King of Poland, under the name of Augustus II, later nicknamed "the Strong", had light-heartedly become a Roman Catholic in order to be elected King of Poland. He appeased the unrest among his horrified subjects with the help of several laws guaranteeing to the Lutheran-Protestant burghers the inviolability of their religion. Matters of contention, which had only recently started wars and mass-flights – such as the cancellation of the Edict of Nantes in 1685, compelling thousands of French Huguenots to emigrate – were obviously no occasion for concern to Augustus. His startling break with the tradition of his country even proved fruitful: since the persecution of the Calvinists towards the end of the sixteenth century, Saxony had become the centre of rigid Lutheran orthodoxy. The Sovereign's change of religion, although dictated by political ambition, discouraged narrow-minded practices. Gifted men saw new paths opening up before them, which until then it had been impossible to tread. The Enlightenment could now spread unhampered.

Although Augustus the Strong immediately started an aggressive war against Sweden, which led to the invasion of Saxony by Charles XII and to the temporary loss of the Polish crown as well as to great sacrifices imposed on the country through taxation, yet the growth of Saxony's economy to new prosperity was nevertheless held up only for a short time. During the thirty-nine years of Augustus' reign twenty-six factories were set up, among them the porcelain factory at Meissen. This compares with twenty-five factories established between 1555 and 1695. It was also during Augustus' reign that all around the impressive town halls in the style of the late Renaissance and the mighty Gothic churches of the Saxon towns the rich burghers' own houses were built with elaborate stucco decorations – witness to the prosperity of that period.

One must not forget, however, that it was above all the luxurious life at the Court which enjoyed this upswing, while national defence and military affairs were severely neglected. Thus the resulting political decline of Saxony was the reverse side of this economic boom.

Augustus the Strong does not seem to have been satisfied with the work of the Dresden goldsmiths during the first years of his reign, since the vessels and utensils in the Green Vaults from about 1700 were all made by Augsburg masters. There is also a whole collection of ruby glasses of various shapes, mainly from South-German glass factories and some even from *Kunckel's* factory at Potsdam. All the mounts, as far as they are distinguishable by marks, were made in Augsburg or Cologne, none in Dresden.

The first jeweller's works commissioned by Augustus the Strong were for jewellery sets of unheard-of costliness. He gave the commission to *Johann Melchior Dinglinger*, probably even before he himself was King of Poland or *Dinglinger* Court Jeweller. From as early as 1692 *Dinglinger* – though still a journeyman and therefore much to the annoyance of the local masters – had made jewellery, caskets, rings and scent bottles for John George IV and for the then Duke Frederic Augustus, evidently sweeping aside all competition. The Saxon goldsmiths of that time used models from Augsburg, the German centre of this art; *Dinglinger* outdid their solid work with the refinement of his forms, his brilliant enamel colours and the unbelievable delicacy of his techniques. The outlines of his earliest works are simple and uncluttered; single diamonds or diamond circles stress the important points of the structure. Most of the enamel is translucent and on the main parts of the surfaces usually shining red or green. The engraved patterns of the gold base produce a lovely velvety shimmer. This gold base, wherever it is left uncovered or combined with enamel of different hues, forms lambrequin-like arches or tendrils in a delicate flat and linear decoration. How charming must such a work have seemed to people who until then had only known surfaces that were bulging and coloured or almost completely hidden under decorations.

Dinglinger's first major work, the coffee-set of gold, which he handed over to the King in December 1701, does not seem to conform with this description of his early work. It is a pyramid-shaped show-piece and looks over-heavy and too richly sculptured, it is not precisely formed and its decoration is not flat and linear. This, however, is the second setting; the master reset the original one in the seventeen-twenties. Originally it was not so tall, more translucent, the moulding was simpler, the structure lighter. The characteristics of *Dinglinger's* early style are to be found only in vessels which underwent no alteration. Of course the jug and the caskets from the later period are more ornate than the small works of the earlier period, which were not intended for show.

With the golden coffee-set and a jewellery set of sapphires – some of which has remained unchanged – *Dinglinger* carried out his first big commission, entrusted to him by the Sovereign. About 1700 the King spent most of his time in Poland partly because of the Northern War, and certainly partly so as to establish firmly his new position as King. No architects or sculptors were called to display the ruler's might in buildings and in series of sculptures at that time in Dresden. Only a Court Jeweller was able to produce transportable objects, works of art which would contribute to the prestige of the Prince as much as architecture or sculpture. It was an ancient and tried practice of founders of dynasties to consolidate the claims of their house through suitably impressive works of art. It was, however, an innovation to confer this task first of all upon a court jeweller.

Dinglinger therefore found himself in a unique position and he was the type of man to respond with unique work. Several surprising new variants of style can be discerned in the golden coffee-set. The pyramid-like pedestal, probably made soon after 1697, is still partly decorated with engraved, strangely flat and stiff scrollwork, which in fact represented a regression of style, to be explained merely by the search for effects through smooth surfaces. In the vessels made around 1700 there are already perfect ribbon-like ornaments of the type made by *Bérain*, perhaps the first of their kind in Germany. Possibly they were suggested to *Dinglinger* by the architectural reconstruction of the principal apartments of the Palace – the throne room and the bed-chamber – by the French architect *Raymond Leplat* in 1698.

The other innovation of consequence in this work is the fact that it follows the Chinoiserie fashion. The cups with covers and the small cups are shaped like East-Asian vessels. Their enamel coating, which imitates porcelain, also follows this fashion, as do the Chinese scenes on the cups with covers, and two engraved panels in the pedestal of the centre piece, and finally the Turkish coffee party sculptured in lacquered wood on the inside.

With the ribbon-like patterns and the Chinoiserie, which can easily be combined into a harmonious decoration, *Dinglinger* determined the style later observed by all Dresden Baroque. All the earlier vessels from the porcelain factory at Meissen make use of both these devices. The refined and lively variations of the French ribbon-like ornaments contrived by *Dinglinger* enlivened the edges of all sorts of works of art made under the auspices of the Court in Dresden, even far into the eighteenth century, and Dresden became one of the principal centres for Chinoiserie in Europe. This became manifest in the works of porcelain and lacquer and in the architecture of the Castle of Pillnitz and the Japanese Palace. *Dinglinger's* "Princely Household of the Great Mogul Aurangzeb" completed in 1708, is probably the first large piece of German Chinoiserie.

It is evident that none of the court jewellers in Dresden could escape the influence of such an outstanding artist and that his work set the standard to which they all aimed. All of them, from *Köhler* and *Döring* to *Taddel* and *Neuber*, who worked in the second half of the century, were in fact his disciples. To him Dresden jewellery owes its almost legendary standard, retained throughout the century.

The Green Vaults contains a large amount of jewellery from the reign of Augustus the Strong. Most of it was made by *Dinglinger* and his workshop and by *Johann Heinrich Köhler*, a distinguished jeweller. Besides these works there are of course works in ivory, wood and silver by *Permoser* and his circle. One of the finest works of the Collection is *Permoser's* "Four Seasons", each one of them skilfully carved from part of a single tusk. *Permoser's* work, like that of the jewellers, is full of vitality, brightness and charm, displayed in a wonderful diversity of forms. It is a difficult style to define, which manages to combine as in *Pöppelmann's Zwinger*, the sumptuousness of the Baroque with an early hint of the Rococo atmosphere.

From the early years of the century dates the acquisition of an odd collection of dwarfs, beggars and grotesque figures, made of irregular pearls and precious stones, strangely enough for the most part not the work of Saxon jewellers. The inventories of the Hall of Preciosities name *Jean Gerardet* of Berlin and *Ferbecq* of Frankfort on the Main as the men from whom they were acquired. No details are known of these outstanding jewellers, probably Huguenots, whose masterpieces are nearly all in the Green Vaults.

Johann Melchior Dinglinger's brother, *Georg Friedrich*, an enameller of note, who died in 1720, had started to make medallions in imitation of classical models in 1710. Soon afterwards a neo-classical late Baroque style came to Dresden, where it was retained with some variations throughout the century. In his later years *Johann Melchior Dinglinger* contributed several pieces in this style, among them the "Obeliscus Augustalis" and the "Apis Altar". This style also appears in the heavy shapes and smooth surfaces of the large jugs of silver gilt, made in 1722 by the Dresden master *Johann Jacob Irminger* with a sculptured decoration by *Balthasar Permoser*.

Works such as these were the last to be purchased as main components for the Collection. As already mentioned, the jewellery sets made for Augustus the Strong were repeatedly altered, decimated or increased. Augustus III for instance bought at the Leipzig Easter Fair of 1742 the forty carat green brilliant for the enormous sum of two hundred thousand Thaler – Raphael's "Sistine Madonna" was acquired for twenty thousand Ducats in 1753. In some of the pieces of jewellery in the Green Vaults the workmanship of the court jewellers and the development of their style may be followed up right to the beginning of the nineteenth century. The last items worth mentioning were added to the Collection at the end of the eighteenth century: the mosaic works in semi-precious stones of Saxon origin by the Court Jeweller *Johann Christian Neuber*.

NOTES

(1) According to the Guide through the Green Vaults, edited by W. Holzhausen, Dresden 1937, p. 5.

(2) O'Byrn, Die Hof-Silberkammer und die Hof-Kellerei zu Dresden, Dresden 1880, p. 101.

(3) Lettres et mémoires de Charles Louis, Baron de Pölnitz, etc., 3rd edition, 1734, Part 1, p. 142. According to the paragraph on Pölnitz in Brockhaus Konversationslexikon, 7th edition, vol. 8, Leipzig 1830, the first edition of the Mémoires was supposed to have been published "at Amsterdam in 1727". Most bibliographies mention only the 3rd edition.

(4) Correspondence of King Augustus II of Poland, State Archives, Dresden, Loc. 2094, No. 185, Fol. 148.

(5) "Information pour le Feltmarchal Comte de Fleming, contenant le Quartier de Fürstenberg au Chateau de Dresden etc." and letter to him by Wackerbart, objecting that the Fürstenberg rooms, not being vaulted, were not sufficiently safe for the archives. Also the first mentioned letter by Flemming to Wackerbart: Matters concerning the Palace at Dresden, 1676–1778, State Archives Dresden, Loc. 773, Vol. IV, Fol. 58, ff.

(6) Th. Graesse, Beschreibender Katalog des K. Grünen Gewölbes, 3rd ed., Dresden 1876, p. VII.

(7) Archives of the Porcelain Factory at Meissen, I. Ae. No. 2, p. 3.

(8) J. G. Keyssler, Neueste Reisen, Hanover 1751, Vol. II, p. 1299: "In another room there are many ingenious time-pieces and objects in gold and silver, moving by themselves ... The lacquer-work on the walls is a good imitation of works in jasper and other stone. The master, called Reinoh, who made it is still living in the Old-Town of Dresden."

(9) J. L. Sponsel, Das Grüne Gewölbe, Leipzig 1925, Vol. I, p. 20.

(10) Files in the Archives of the Green Vaults.

(11) Heinz Ladendorf, Andreas Schlüter, Berlin 1935, p. 145, Note 32; H. G. Franz, Zacharias Longuelune und die Bauwerke des 18. Jahrhunderts in Dresden, Berlin 1953, p. 12, ff.

(12) Account from the Archives of the Green Vaults, dated 13th March 1724, concerning 160 Thaler, reduced by the Court's Building Office to 120 Thaler; published in "Neue Museumskunde", Vol. 8, part 4, 1965 by Gerhard Glaser, Das Grüne Gewölbe im Dresdener Residenzschloss.

(13) In 1962 an inscription was discovered on the reverse of a board, which makes it possible to fix the date of the decoration of the Enamel Room after 1727/1728: "Johannes Lang, joiner's son from Blaubeyren in Württemberg made this pillar at the end of 1727." "Christ's Blood and Justice are my jewels and coat of honour. In these I hope I shall stand before God when this and everything else will perish; Amen." Discovered and published by Gerhard Glaser. l.c., p. 298.

(14) Gerhard Glaser, l.c., p. 295, was able to trace this style of the decoration back to sketches for ceilings by Nicolas Loir 1624–1679.

(15) O'Byrn, l.c., pp. 1–21.

(16) These traces of a decoration in gold were discovered by Professor Dr. Hahnloser, Bern.

(17) Forberger, R., Die Manufaktur in Sachsen vom Ende des 16. bis zum Anfang des 19. Jahrhunderts, Berlin, 1958, p. 16.

BIBLIOGRAPHY

Anonymous, (Freiherr Friedrich August O'Byrn), Die Hof-Silberkammer und die Hof-Kellerei zu Dresden. Dresden 1880.

Anonymous, Beschreibung des Grünen Gewölbes in Dresden, dem noch beygefüget einige kurtze Zusätze zu Herrn Heckels Beschreibung des Königsteins, Franckfurt und Leipzig 1737.

Beutel, T., Churfürstl. Sächsischer stets grünender hoher Cedern-Wald. Dresden 1671.

Catalogue: 400 Jahre Dresdener Kunstsammlungen. Dresden 1960.

Dassdorf, K. W. Beschreibung der vorzüglichsten Merkwürdigkeiten der Churfürstlichen Residenz-stadt Dresden. Dresden 1782.

Doering, I., Des Augsburger Patriciers Philipp Heinhofer Reisen nach Innsbruck und Dresden. Wien 1901.

Erbstein, J. and A., Das Königliche Grüne Gewölbe zu Dresden. Dresden 1884.

Fischer, W., Die Mineralogie in Sachsen von Agricola bis Werner. Dresden 1939.

Forberger, R., Die Manufaktur in Sachsen vom Ende des 16. bis zum Anfang des 19. Jahrhunderts. Berlin 1958.

Glaser, G., Das Grüne Gewölbe im Dresdener Residenzschloss, in: Neue Museumskunde, Vol. VIII, part 4, 1965.

Graesse, J. G. T., Beschreibender Katalog des K. Grünen Gewölbes zu Dresden. Dresden 1872.

–. Das Grüne Gewölbe zu Dresden. Hundert Lichtdrucktafeln, Verlag Paul Bette, Berlin without date.

Hantzsch, V., Beiträge zur älteren Geschichte der Kurf. Kunstkammer in Dresden. Neues Archiv für sächsische Geschichte und Altertumskunde, Vol. XXIII, Dresden 1902.

Holzhausen, W., Führer durch das Grüne Gewölbe in Dresden. Dresden 1937.

–. Lage und Rekonstruktion der kurfürstlichen Kunstkammer ... Repertorium für Kunstwissen-schaften, Vol. 48, Berlin, Leipzig 1927.

Holzhausen, W., Kesting, E., Prachtgefäße, Geschmeide, Kabinettstücke, Goldschmiedekunst in Dres-den. Tübingen 1966.

Iccander, Das fast auf dem höchsten Gipfel seiner Vollkommenheit und Glückseligkeit prangende königliche Dresden. Dresden 1726.

Keyssler, J. G., Neueste Reisen, Vol. II, Hanover 1751.

Landsberg, A. B. von, Das Grüne Gewölbe in Dresden, 1st ed., Dresden 1831.

–. Das Grüne Gewölbe zu Dresden. Eine Folge ausgewählter Kunstwerke dieser Sammlung nach den Zeichnungen von R. Seidemann und F. Mohn, ed. by Ludwig Gruner. Dresden 1862.

Menzhausen, J., Catalogue of the exhibition "Der Menschheit bewahrt" (Preserved for Mankind), chapter on the Green Vaults, Dresden 1961.

–. Das Grüne Gewölbe, in: Weltstädte der Kunst: Dresden. Leipzig and Munich 1965.

Seidlitz, W. von, Die Kunst in Dresden vom Mittelalter bis zur Neuzeit. 4 Vols., Dresden 1920 to 1922.

Seydewitz, R. and M., Die Dresdener Kunstschätze. Dresden 1960.

Sponsel, J. L., Das Grüne Gewölbe zu Dresden, 4 Vols., Leipzig from 1925 to 1932.

–. Führer durch das Grüne Gewölbe. Dresden 1921.

–. Der Zwinger, die Hoffeste und die Schlossbaupläne zu Dresden, 2 Vols., Dresden 1924.

–. Das Grüne Gewölbe nach seiner Erweiterung und Neuaufstellung, in: Mitteilungen aus den sächsi-schen Kunstsammlungen, Vol. V., Dresden and Berlin 1914.

Weck, A., Der Chur-fürstlich Sächsischen weitberuffenen Residentz und Haupt-Vestung Dresden Beschreib: und Vorstellung, Nürnberg 1680.

COMMENTS ON THE ILLUSTRATIONS

3 Supporting Figure of a Drinking Vessel, known as Gryphon-Claw
Detail of Plate 4, above, left.

4 Four Gryphon-Claws
Horn, mounted in silver gilt.
Above, left:
On the rim around the lip two shields with coats of arms: on one a strutting lion with two tails, against a red background, the other is divided crosswise and was filled with red enamel. There are two more shields, showing half-length figures of Christ giving the blessing and of the Virgin holding a book and flanked by two shields with stylized blossoms. On the underside of the lid is a shield with a hind lying under trees, and a squirrel. There is a supporting figure gripping a tree-trunk with its hands. On two bands around the tree is an engraved inscription: *halt veste uns komen geste* (hold fast, guests are coming to us). Transverse hoops on the goblet are decorated with stylized tendrils with blossoms. Under the hoop at the back are two lions as supporting figures. The left one – as seen from the front – was added after 1920 by the Dresden goldsmith *Eckert*. The mount of the point of the horn is decorated with engraved foliage amidst spiral-like bands. Above these is an imaginary building; behind city-walls stands a cruciform chapel, accessible by way of the spandrels and an oblique central tower.
German, early fifteenth century.
Height 34 cm., length 48 cm.; Inv. No. IV, 333.
Right:
Shields with a stylized ram's horn motif and traces of red enamel on the background are soldered onto the rim of the lip, to both the transverse hoops and to the point. The coats of arms on them are supposed to be those of the Lords of Salza in Thuringia. Two silver-gilt human legs, hinged and movable, support the goblet. The lid and point are missing.
German, fourteenth century.
Height 31 cm., length 47 cm.; Inv. No. IV, 331.
Below, left:
The crosswise interlaced Gothic minuscules "a" and "e" are engraved on the rim of the lip. The supporting figure is an embossed gryphon; its wings are curved upwards to act as a transverse hoop. A castle stands on the point of the horn. Above the entrance is a bay-window with a door-keeper looking out of it. On top of the tower stand three guards.
German, early fifteenth century; lid: late sixteenth century. Nuremberg hall mark; master's mark of *Jobst Müllner*, R. 3847.
Height 29 cm., length 23.5 cm.; Inv. No. IV, 269.
Right:
Foliage and fleurons are engraved on the rim of the lip, the transverse hoop and the point. The supporting figure is an embossed eagle, standing on a horizontal piece of branch. The eagle's left wing has been broken off. The support at the back is shaped like two lion's feet. The inside of the claw is lined with silver, engraved with a pattern of vine-tendrils and grapes.
German, late fourteenth century. Height 22.5 cm., length 25 cm.;
Inv. No. IV, 338.

5 Three Gothic Vessels of Rock Crystal

Rock crystal mounted in silver gilt, partly enamelled.

Left:

Goblet of Queen Edwiga of Poland (1384–1399), a twelve-sided vessel of rock crystal with a peg on which to fasten the mount of the handle. Symmetrical designs of fleurons and foliage are engraved on the stand and on the handle. An inscription in black enamel on the ring below the cup reads: *hedwig · cyfu · scadat · q · ctulit · istu · psul · obmita · wenceslai · s gt a digna · polonor · regina · supna · polor* (May Edwiga, the exalted Queen of Poland, deserving of heaven, drink from this goblet, which the bishop gave her for her merits, so pleasing to St. Wenceslaus). (Deciphered by M. Gebarowicz, Dawna Szuka II,1, Lvov 1939, made available through the kindness of Professor Adam Bochnak, Krakow). Escutcheons with the coats of arms of Hungary-Anjou in enamel are on the stand and on the lid; on the handle is an escutcheon with a monogram formed of two letters "M" interlaced rectangularly against a background of blue enamel. On the vault of the lid are two similar monograms, but without any coloured background. According to Gebarowicz this is the monogram of Martha and Mary as personifications of *vita activa* and *vita contemplativa*. A frieze of lilies is chiselled into the rim of the lip; on top of the lid is an enamelled circular shield with the Polish eagle. The wreath of lilies surrounding it is not chiselled, nor is that on the rim of the lid. The outlines only of a frieze of lilies are engraved in the panels of the lid; the lid as a whole looks unfinished. Gebarowicz suggests that the mount was made by the Krakow master of the Royal seal of King Wladyslaw Jagiello, because both the eagle on the lid and the inscription correspond to that seal. Probably the work was interrupted at the sudden death of the twenty-five year-old Queen and was eventually finished in a careless manner. The goblet is included in an inventory of possessions of the Wettinian family, covering the years from 1541 to 1662. There are several old cracks in the crystal of the vessel.

Probably French, fourteenth century; mount made in Krakow, late fourteenth century.

Height 24 cm.;

Inv. No. V, 294.

Centre:

Twelve-sided Vessel with a peg for the mount of the handle. On the concave surface of the stand is an ornament of enamelled blossoms and painted leaves. The mount of the handle is shaped like tracery. There is a frieze of opaque red and translucent blue and green enamel around the rim of the lid and a similar one on the top of the lid, crowned by a wreath of pearls and finally by a painted branch of leaves. On the stand, opposite the handle, is a crozier with a coat of arms soldered onto it, showing a black lion with a crown on a background of silver.

Probably French, fourteenth century.

Height 17 cm.;

Inv. No. V, 208.

Right:

Twelve-sided Vessel, slightly flattened at either side. The stand is hexagonal and curved, its base of tiny openwork. The spout represents a dragon and its base is fixed into the vessel through a hole drilled into it mid-way up. On the reverse side of the stand, covered with blue enamel, and on the lid are Gothic letters in gold. A flower on the reverse side of the stand, and the point surmounting the lid, are in the same blue enamel.

Vessel: French (?), fourteenth century; mount: fifteenth century. Height 21 cm.; Inv. No. V, 276.

6 Plaque with Relief of the Apostles John and Paul

Ivory, mounted in silver, parcel gilt.

Figures and architecture of the platform are depicted in high-relief. Both apostles stand obliquely, presenting the right side of their bodies. They hold the gospel books in their left hands; they are therefore shown in perspective. St. John lifts his right hand to administer the blessing, St. Paul turns his head to the right. Vertical inscriptions are incised besides their haloes: "*A Joannes o Theolog. O Agios Paulos*". A horizontal inscription in relief reads: "The instrument of God (Paul) discusses with the chaste man (John) how to protect the Emperor Constantine from harm". The front of the mount is gilded; both the front and the back edge are framed by bead–mouldings soldered onto the mount.

Formerly in the Church of San Giovanni in Verdura in Padua, the plaque came to the Green Vaults in 1855 from the chapel of the Taschenberg Palace in Dresden. Closely similar Ivories are in Vienna and Venice.

Byzantine, tenth century. Measurements: 25 × 13.4 cm.; Inv. No. II, 52.

7 The Crucifixion

Relief of wood by *Peter Dell*, signed "PD 1528". Some traces of the original mount are preserved on the clothing. For the chief figures *Dell* used works by his master, *Hans Leinberger*, as models. He carved the "Crucifixion" for Duke Henry at the same time as a "Resurrection", while staying in Saxony. Included in the inventory of 1587, the earliest of the Cabinet of Curiosities.

Measurements: 39.5 × 50.5 cm.; Inv. No. I, 49.

8 Tree of Jesse

Silver, parcel gilt and sharks' teeth.

The Virgin, with a crown on her head, sits with the Child inside a flower with a long stem in front of a shark's tooth, known as a viper's tongue. The embossed pedestal represents a rock; there Abraham is asleep, while the dragon creeps out of its cave. Something is missing in front of the dragon – perhaps a figure of St. George. The cast figure of Abraham has been screwed on at a later date. The pedestal was not originally made to carry this Tree of Jesse, and appears somewhat older. The flower and the figure of the Virgin are cast by the same master as Abraham.

Acquired 1876. There was a similar work in the Cabinet of Curiosities.

German, late fifteenth century. Height 19.5 cm.; Inv. No. IV, 108.

9 Three Gothic Vessels of Semi-Precious Stone

Amethyst, jasper, and noble serpentine mounted in silver gilt and copper.

Left:

Eleven-sided Vessel in red and white agate with amethysts embedded in it. Naked men and women alternate with each other on the base; they are riding on lions followed by winged dragons; at the upper end of the handle is a similar couple riding on a lion, at the lower end are two lions. Each pair of animals holds a heart. There is a peg for the mount of the handle; on top of the handle is a kneeling angel in relief. There are surprisingly traces of champlevé enamel on the gilding of the lid. The point is missing. All the work of the mount is coarse.

Mount made in Burgundy (?), fourteenth century.

Height 14 cm.; Inv. No. IV, 343.

Small Goblet with Lid, yellow-red jasper with oblique fluting. The mount is in copper, the frieze of finials cast in gilded bronze. The point is broken off.

Fifteenth century. Height 22.5 cm.; Inv. No. V, 488.

Right:

Round Vessel with Cover, made of noble serpentine. There is a peg for the mount of the handle. On the crown of the cover is a cast ornament of masks in leaves, and in the centre amidst these a revolving shield with stylized blossoms engraved into both its surfaces.

Probably German, late fifteenth century. Height 15.5 cm.; Inv. No. V, 404.

10 Above: Two Bowls made of Coins in the shape of a Roman *patera*

Gold and silver gilt.

Left:

Silver Bowl, gilded and embossed, made with twenty-five Roman denarii of the Consulate. In the centre a Greek coin with the head of Alexander the Great. The stamped silver of the coins has not been gilded. There is an inscription in black champlevé enamel which reads: *dona praesentis cape laetus horae.*

Acquired 1865. Italian (?), early sixteenth century. Diameter 20.5 cm.; Inv. No. IV, 44.

Right:

Bowl of Olmützer, engraved bowl in gold with twenty-two Roman gold-coins (some of them copies). In the centre a chiselled and cast gold medal with a genius and the following inscriptions, on the front: GENIO LIBERO Q PATRI, on the reverse side: AUG OLOM SIBI ET GRATAE POSTERITATI MDVIII (Augustin Olmützer to himself and his estimated successors, 1508). Augustin Kesenbrot, known as Olmützer, was chancellor of King Vladislaw II of Hungary. He is said to have presented this bowl in 1508 to the learned Danubian Society, an association of Humanists for the furtherance of arts and science. The inscription on the outer ring reads: "PHOEBIGENUM. SACRATA. COHORS. ET. MYSTICUS. ORDO. HAC. PATERA. BACCHI. MUNERA. LARGA. FERANT. PROCUL. HINC. PROCUL. ESTE. PROPHANI". (May the holy band of Apollo's sons and their holy order lavishly sacrifice to Bacchus with this bowl. May the non-initiated stay away). The bowl went from the principal church at Olmütz to Russia and was acquired there by Augustus the Strong in approximately 1700.

The engraving is somewhat coarse; it contains motifs from etchings by *Nicoletto da Modena.*

Hungarian (?), prior to 1508. Diameter 18.3 cm., weight 802 gramm; Inv. No. IV, 40.

10 Below: Reverse Side of the Bowl of Olmützer

11 Large Flask with Handle

Silver gilt.

On the disk-like body two embossed scenes: five commanders besieging a town, and a peasant on horseback with a prisoner of war in front of a beleaguered town. Above each of these scenes is the coat of arms of the Electorate of Saxony. The decoration contains South-German and Italian motifs; the embossed landscapes appear to be influenced by the Danubian School. It is not a work of the first quality.

From the territory of Austria-Hungary after 1530. Height including handle 81 cm.; Inv. No. IV, 253.

12 Small Writing Case

Silver, parcel gilt, enamel, velvet, silk, rock crystal, ebony.

The case is made up of cast panels. The allegorical figure of Philosophy is embossed; on the tablet in her hand is an inscription which reads: *Litere rebus memorē caducis | Suscitāt vitā, monumenta fida | Artiũ condũt, revocāt ad auras | Lapsa sub umbras MCLXII.* (Science with the help of memory recalls to life what is ephemeral, erects lasting monuments to the arts, calls back to light what has fallen into darkness, 1562). On the reverse: *tabula Phythagorea,* a square with the figures from one to ten, forming a vertical and a horizontal multiplication table; below it, some examples of the first four rules of arithmetic.

The narrow side of the case, nearest to the feet of the figure, can be lifted off. Inside are four little drawers of ebony, lined with silk and gilded silver-foil, into which a design of moresques in lacquer-colours has been impressed. There are also an inkpot and a pot for blotting sand, both of silver.

The case came to the Cabinet of Curiosities in 1623 from the estate of Sophia, widow of Elector Christian I.

By *Wenzel Jamnitzer,* Nuremberg 1562. Nuremberg hall mark; master's mark: *Wenzel Jamnitzer,* R. 3832. Measurements: 31 × 24 × 11 cm.; Inv. No. V, 599.

13 Rose-Water Basin and Jug

Silver gilt, mother of pearl, wood, copper.

The core of the basin is wood, its reverse side lacquered in bright red; the body of the jug is copper. Both objects with their covering of mother of pearl are of oriental origin, but their silver-gilt mounts are German, probably by a Nuremberg master, about 1530.

Basin: diameter 56 cm.; Inv. No. IV, 181; Jug: height 29 cm.; Inv. No. IV, 256.

14 Leaping Unicorn

Brass-work by *Hans Reisinger* of Augsburg.

Acquired from the master himself in 1589 (see inventory of 1595 of the Cabinet of Curiosities). Height 37.8 cm.; Inv. No. IX, 51.

15 Three Goblets of Rock Crystal

Rock crystal, silver gilt, enamel.

Left:

Goblet of Rock Crystal, probably cut in Freiburg im Breisgau. On the mount a Moresque ornament in champlevé enamel and a wreath of flowers painted in cold colours around the knob.

Augsburg hall mark R. 124; master's mark HNS (the letters in ligature) R. 426. About 1570 to 1580. Height 40 cm.; Inv. No. V, 180.

Centre:

Goblet of Rock Crystal; cut from rock crystal, with metal mount, from Freiburg im Breisgau.

Hall mark R. 2108; master's mark R. 2124 *(Burkart Frauenfeld?).* About 1570–1580. Height 27 cm.; Inv. No. V, 187.

Right:

The Nesen-Luther Goblet; the cup without any mount, probably cut in the thirteenth century, was given by Martin Luther to his friend Wilhelm Nesen (1493–1524), a Professor at Wittenberg;

his brother, burgomaster of Zittau, who died in 1560, had a mount made for the goblet. The lid is in the shape of a cylinder, and the crests of the families Rosenheim, von Milde, von Bischofswerda, all related to the Nesens, are painted in enamel on it; on top is that of the Nesen family itself, cast in silver and gilded. The last of the family bequested the goblet in 1793 to the Cabinet of Curiosities.

Mount by *Christoff Ritter* I, master in 1547. Nuremberg hall mark; master's mark R. 3880. Prior to 1560. Height 39 cm.; Inv. No. V, 188.

16 Chalice and small Wine Jug for Holy Communion

Gold, gems, enamel.

The Chalice. The cup is embossed, all the other parts are cast. It is an outstanding work of art, both for its moulding and for its enamel decoration. A relief of the Crucifixion with Mary and John is soldered to the foot, on the opposite side the coat of arms of Count Johann Gebhard of Mansfeld, Archbishop and Elector of Cologne from 1558–1562.

Presumably made in Cologne. Height 19.5 cm., weight 788 gramm; Inv. No. IV, 42.

The small Jug. The letter "V" (*vinum*) in black enamel, soldered onto the front of the jug, indicates the function of the vessel. Its general shape, the wreath of lilies around the shaft and the dragon's head on the handle are reminiscent of the Gothic style. In this, in the colour of its gold and the inferior quality of the champlevé enamel and the scrollwork the jug differs from the chalice. On the lid is a square formed of four diamonds.

German, about 1550. Height 16.5 cm.; Inv. No. IV, 41.

17 Drinking Cup, Kovsh, of Tsar Ivan the Terrible

Gold with niello, sapphires, pearls.

There is an inscription around the rim reading: "By the grace of God and by order of the Supreme Ruler, the Tsar and Grand Duke Ivan Vasilievich of All-Russia, of Vladimir, Moscow, Novgorod, the Tsar of Kazan, the Tsar of Astrakhan, the Ruler of Pskov and the Grand Duke of Smolensk, Tver, Zagorsk, Perm, Viatka, Bolgar and others, the Ruler and Grand Duke of Novgorod Oblast, of Chernigov, Ryazan, Polotsk, Rostov, Yaroslavl, Belozersk, of the Country at the Udora, of Obdorsk, of Kondinsk and of the Districts of the Siberian Country and the North Country, and Ruler of the Livonian Country and others." On the reverse side of the round base of the cup is a further inscription in niello: "The Sovereign ordered this cup to be made of gold from Polotsk, when he conquered that town his true inheritance, on 15th February 1563." On the inside the base is decorated in niello with the Russian double-headed eagle worked in a West-European style. The elongated shape of the cup is in accordance with the traditions of Moldavia. The cup was a present from Tsar Peter the Great to Augustus the Strong.

Russian, after 1563. Length 23 cm., weight 1015 gramm; Inv. No. IV, 43.

18 Three Goblets made of Coconuts

Silver gilt, coconut shells.

Left:

Coconut Goblet with lid crowned by a putto, representing an angel holding an escutcheon. On the lower part of the shield is a horizontal hatching, above it is a tree with a flower on each side of its top and also on each side of its roots. The cup is lined with silver gilt. Inside the lid is a slightly curved shield with the same coat of arms as that on top and with the date 1540. The coat of arms of the Dukes of Saxony is chased on the rim of the stand.

German, 1540. Height 27 cm.; Inv. No. IV, 336.

Centre:

Coconut Goblet with three reliefs carved into the shell, showing scenes from the story of the Prodigal Son; woodcuts by *H. S. Beham* (1500–1550) were used as models. On the base of the cup is a medallion-like ornament with the head of Christ seen in profile; his face and neck are not gilt. Around it are the words: EGO SUM JHESUS A ET Ω.

Nuremberg (?), about 1560. Height 28.5 cm.; Inv. No. IV, 330.

Right:

Coconut Goblet. The shaft is formed by a trunk, around which a snake is winding itself. On the branch is an escutcheon, divided into four parts: eagles and two birds standing opposite each other holding a heart in their beaks.

Without marks. German, third quarter of the 16th century. Height 25 cm.; Inv. No. IV, 323.

19 Three Works of Rock Crystal

Rock crystal, gold, enamel, gems.

Left:

Tankard with Lid, engraved with figures of mediocre quality representing allegories of the senses: taste, sight, smell and touch. Mounted in gold with emeralds and rubies. Handle and body of the tankard are in one piece. The top of the lid and the knob on one of the hinges are restorations of the mid-seventeenth century.

German (?), after 1600. Height 20 cm.; Inv. No. V, 173.

Centre:

Orpheus and the Animals in a Sphere of Rock Crystal. The shaft and the foot are of rock crystal, covered with an ornamental trellis in enamelled gold. At the top is a clock in a smaller sphere, also of rock crystal; on it is a horizontal ring, showing like a dial the figures of a clock. A figure of Saturn points the hours using a spear like the hand of a clock. Below the group of Orpheus is an inscription reading: *Orpheus kunt lieblich hofieren den Voeglen und wilden Thieren + das sie wurden milt und sanftmietig und sprungen frolig und gietig.* (Orpheus knew how to pay court to the birds and wild beasts and to charm them so that they became mild and gentle and leaped about happily and in a friendly mood.) There is a comparable work in the *Kunsthistorisches Museum* (Museum of Fine Arts) in Vienna.

South-German, early seventeenth century. Height 21.5 cm.; Inv. No. VI, 19.

Right:

Goblet of Rock Crystal. Mount of gold and enamel, decorated with rubies. The vessel was made in Freiburg im Breisgau, the mount in Southern Germany, after 1600.

Height 27 cm.; Inv. No. V, 172.

20 Galley of Rock Crystal

Rock crystal, gold, emeralds, rubies, enamel.

The stand is formed of two dragons back to back with scroll-shaped wings. Several scenes are engraved on the hull: the "Rape of Europa", the "Deliverance of Andromeda", the "Rape of Helena" and the "Siege of Troy". Aloft on a kind of small roof perched on top at one end of the galley is the Danish (?) flag. The mounts of the roof and of the decoration on the reverse side seem to have been renovated about 1600. Inside, on a transverse band of gold, is a cartouche topped by a crown with the letters "AR" on a red background, the monogram of Augustus the Strong; this was restored in 1705. A similar galley was bought in 1601 by Elector Christian II from *Ambrogio Saracco*, and yet another one – a present from Emperor Ferdinand II to Elector John George I – was noted by Hainhofer in 1629 in the Pavilion on the Jungfernbastei in Dresden. Workshop of the brothers *Saracchi*, Milan, late sixteenth century. Measurements: 37 × 44 × 27 cm.; Inv. No. V, 185.

21 Flask and Jug of Rock Crystal

Rock crystal, gold, emeralds, rubies, enamel.
Flask, decorated with scenes from the story of Noah, engraved after a sketch by *Annibale Fontana*. The inventory of the treasury of 1588 mentions the flask, which at that time had a stopper. The base was made separately.
Workshop of the brothers *Saracchi*, Milan, about 1580. Height 31.5 cm.; Inv. No. V, 186.
Jug; the body of a grotesque figure of the devil is shown in high-relief on the reverse side of the jug; the head and wings are additions in gold.
Milan, about 1580. Height 24.7 cm.; Inv. No. V, 306.

22 Standing Mirror on Column of Rock Crystal

Rock crystal, mirror glass, gold, enamel, silver gilt, gems, pearls.
According to the inventory of the Cabinet of Curiosities of 1587 a present from Duke Emanuel Philibert of Savoy, died 1580. The column and the exceedingly well sculptured frame are jeweller's work from Milan, about 1580. The profile of the silver-gilt frame has been filed away so as to fit the plastic gold ornament on to it. In 1724 the Court Jeweller *Johann Heinrich Köhler* restored most of the work to make it suitable for exhibition in the Green Vaults. He put in new mirror glass on both sides and possibly renovated the frame as well. Stand and frame are decorated with trimmings similar in design to those used on clothing. These ornaments as well as the silver-gilt stand with inlaid plates of rock crystal may have been made after 1580, when the mirror was probably restored for the first time.
Height 77 cm.; Inv. No. V, 171.

23 Crucifix of Rock Crystal

Rock crystal, gold, enamel, silver gilt, gems.
Christ's body and the legend are engraved. Lily-like ornaments are attached to the ends of the beams of the Cross and held there by disks decorated on both sides with the symbols of the Evangelists in gold and enamel. The engraving of the crystal and also the jeweller's plastic work are very fine, evidently from Milan about 1580. The gold and enamel figures of Mary and John are sculptured in a more primitive technique; they are stuck on spikes soldered into the scrollwork ornaments. The mount of the foot and that of the baluster are silver-gilt, made about 1600.
The crucifix was bought in 1602 from the Dresden goldsmith *Gabriel Gipfel*, died 1617. A study of work by this master leads one to assume that he may have made both the little figures and the mounts of the coloured stones on the foot, even, perhaps, the mount of the whole lower part of the work. Height 41.5 cm.; Inv. No. V, 178.

24 Top: Six Vessels of Stone

Heliotrope, green jasper, lapis lazuli, chalcedony-agates.

Above, left:

Hexagonal Bowl of Heliotrope, mount of gold and enamel.

Italian, late sixteenth century. Height 10.7 cm.; Inv. No. V, 24.

Centre:

Oval Bowl with Cover; heliotrope, mount of gold and enamel.

Milan (?), late sixteenth century. Height 9.3 cm.; Inv. No. V, 16.

Right:

Bowl of Green Jasper, mounted in gold and enamel and decorated with diamonds, emeralds, rubies and one pearl. Neptune sits on the rim and thrusts his trident at a dolphin lying in the bowl. The jeweller's work is excellent. The figure "C5", surmounted by a crown, is engraved into the base of the bowl. The bowl may therefore have belonged to the treasury of King Christian V of Denmark.

Milan (?), late sixteenth century. Height 14 cm.; Inv. No. VI, 36.

Below, left:

Round Bowl of Chalcedony with mount of gold and enamel. The handles begin at the open-work stand and end in masks of fauns fixed to the rim of the bowl.

Florence (?), late sixteenth century. Came to the Green Vaults in 1734. Height 8.3 cm.; Inv. No. V, 114.

Centre:

Jug of Lapis Lazuli. The jug is not mounted. Body and handle are in one piece. The portion below the ring round the shaft has been stuck on. The design of the jug is reminiscent of sketches by *Bernardo Buontalenti.*

Probably Florentine, late sixteenth century. Height 27 cm.; Inv. No. V, 56.

Right:

Shallow Bowl of Brownish Chalcedony-Agate, mounted in gold and enamel.

Milan (?), late sixteenth century. Height 5.5 cm.; Inv. No. V, 490.

24 Bottom: Three Vessels of Noble Serpentine

Noble serpentine, mounts of gold and silver gilt.

Left:

Cup-Like Bowl in enamelled mount of gold. Under the rim of the lid is an inscription which reads: *vas ex jaspide antiquum Alexandriae Aegypti repertum tali ornamento dignum.*

The bowl is ancient, the mount is probably Italian. Late sixteenth century. Height 7 cm.; Inv. No. V, 383.

Centre:

Small Bowl mounted in gold.

The mount about 1600. Height 3.7 cm.; Inv. No. V, 382.

Right:

Bowl with Lid in silver-gilt mount. On the inside of the lid is a disk with the coats of arms of Saxony and Denmark and the date 1572. The bowl probably belonged to Anna, wife of Elector Augustus.

Diameter 10.5 cm.; Inv. No. V, 384.

25 Three Vessels of Rock Crystal

Rock crystal, mounts of gold and enamel.

Left:

Small Quatrefoil Goblet with rings of gold and enamel around the shaft.

Milan (?), about 1600. Height 15 cm.;

Inv. No. V, 337.

Centre:

Four-sided Casket with Lid, mounted in gold and enamel.

Prague (?), about 1600. Height 16 cm.;

Inv. No. V, 227.

Right:

Small Barrel, mounted in gold and enamel.

Probably Prague, early seventeenth century. Height 15.7 cm.;

Inv. No. V, 205.

26 Large Bowl of Limoges Enamel

Enamel on copper.

The Emperor, the Pope, priests and princes are pleading with the Woman of the Apocalypse.

Signed on the reverse side "Courtois", that is *Martial Courteys* of Limoges.

Late sixteenth century. Measurements: 41 × 55 cm.;

Inv. No. III, 8.

27 Two Flasks of Opaline

Glass, silver gilt, enamel.

Left:

Opaline Flask. The figure of the knight on the stopper holds a shield with the coat of arms in enamel of Eberhard von Stein, abbot of Kempten, 1571–1584. A similar coat of arms and the head of an ox with the date 1574 are painted in champlevé enamel on each side of the flask.

The flask is Venetian. On the mount is the hall mark of Kaufbeuren and the master's mark R.2637.

Height 48 cm.;

Inv. No. IV, 179.

Right:

Venetian Flask of Opaline

Simple mount of silver gilt, probably South-German, about 1600. Height 35 cm.;

Inv. No. IV, 205.

28 Five Tankards of Serpentine

Serpentine in silver-gilt mounts.

The crest of the Frese family from Emden is to be seen on the ring around the left tankard.

Hall mark of Emden framed by the figures 8 and 9; the mount was therefore made in 1590.

Master's mark "FM" (letters in ligature). Probably by *Franz Muntinck*, master 1576. Acquired 1927.

The other four tankards are in the light grey serpentine of Saxony. Two of them have no handles; the coats of arms of Saxony and of Denmark are engraved upon them, that is those of Elector Augustus and of his Danish wife Anna. Doubtless, the tankards were made for the Court. The

mounts of all four of these Saxon tankards are by the Dresden master *Urban Schneeweiss*, 1536–1600.
Dresden hall mark; master's mark R. 1726.
From left to right: Height 18 cm.; Inv. No. 1927/4.
Height 29 cm.; Inv. No. V, 380. Height 28 cm.; Inv. No. V, 398.
Height 17 cm.; Inv. No. V, 388. Height 31.5 cm.;
Inv. No. V, 390.

29 Three Embossed Goblets from Nuremberg

Silver gilt.
From Left to Right:
Double Goblet, embossed.
By *Andreas Rosa*, master 1599. Nuremberg hall mark; master's mark R. 4100. Height of each goblet 35 cm.; Inv. Nos. IV, 296 and IV, 301.
Embossed Goblet with design of Grapes. The shaft represents a vintager; on the lid rests a bunch of flowers painted in cold colours.
Nuremberg hall mark; master's mark 4045/55. Probably by *Hanns Beutmüller*, master 1588, died 1622. Early seventeenth century. Height 77 cm.; Inv. No. IV, 12.
Embossed Goblet with Twisted Design.
By *Peter Wiber*, master 1603, died 1641. Nuremberg hall mark; master's mark R. 4119. Height 62 cm.; Inv. No. IV, 297.

30 Large Jewellery Chest

Silver, parcel gilt, mother of pearl, velvet, silk, glass, core of wood, gems, pearls.
On the lid are fragments of a clock and of a reclining figure in relief, which originally pointed out the hours on a revolving dial. Drawers, lined with silk, velvet, pearls and gems, are fitted into the chest. The chest came to the Cabinet of Curiosities in 1589. A drawing in Leningrad shows that the sketch for the chest was by *Wenzel Jamnitzer*, 1508–1585, who also made many of the cast parts.
Nuremberg hall mark; master's mark R. 4030 of *Nicolaus Schmidt*, master 1582, died 1609.
Measurements: 50 × 54 × 36 cm.; Inv. No. IV, 115.

31 Inside of Lid of the large Jewellery Chest

The translucent lacquer on the relief-figures in silver has been perfectly preserved.

32 Four Objects with Limoges Enamel

Enamel on copper.
Jug with triumphal procession of Diana in enamel. Signed "J.C.", the signature of a member of the *Court*-family of Limoges.
Late sixteenth century. Height 28 cm.; Inv. No. III, 6.
Plate with picture of the Virgin and Child in a garden. On the front of the plate are the letters "J E W" in gold (the names to which these letters refer have not yet been ascertained); on a white band are the words *Vita. Divae. Mariae. Virginis*.
Signed "J.C.", the signature of a member of the *Court*-family of Limoges.
Late sixteenth century. Diameter 24 cm.; Inv. No. III, 25.

Small Casket, mounted in gilded bronze. The labours of Hercules are depicted in enamel on the plates of which the casket is composed.

In the manner of *Colin Nouailher*, mid-sixteenth century. Measurements: 11.5 × 19 × 12.5 cm.; Inv. No. III, 264.

Salt-Cellar with six classical deities, and in the hollowed-out part the head of a Roman warrior. Signed "J.L." by *Jean I. Limosin*, about 1600. Acquired 1871. Height 9 cm.; Inv. No. III, 1.

33 Jug and Two Plates of Latticinio Glass

Latticinio glass.

Pieces from a set which includes a large basin.

Venetian, late sixteenth century. Height of jug 34 cm.; Inv. No. V, 161; Diameter of plates 17.5 cm.; Inv. No. V, 162.

34 Glass Plate with Figures of Jupiter and Juno

Glass, frame of pear-tree wood.

An incunabulum; one of the earliest examples of the art of engraving glass. Comparison with similar works in Prague suggests that the plate is one of the earliest works of *Caspar Lehmann*. The model for the design was a drawing by *B. Spranger*. Acquired for the Cabinet of Curiosities in 1590.

Measurements with frame: 20.5 × 17.8 cm.; Inv. No. VI, 70.

35 Two Jugs of Faience

Faience, silver gilt.

Left:

Faience Jug, blue glaze with white speckles. Perhaps of oriental origin, originally it had a long neck, now broken off. Mount by the Dresden goldsmith *Martin Borisch*, master 1613, died 1649.

Dresden hall mark; master's mark R. 1749. Height 26.3 cm.; Inv. No. IV, 207.

Right:

Faience Jug, violet glaze with white speckles. The jug appears to be made of English faience, known as Malling-ware. On the rim of the lip are the interlaced letters "AA", the monogram of Elector Augustus and his wife Anna. Below the ring around the foot are the letters "F.C." Mount German, about 1560. Height 27 cm.; Inv. No. IV, 279.

36 Three Saxon Goblets

Silver gilt.

Left:

Cylindrical Goblet, decorated with fifteen Saxon coats of arms inserted into the surface, while the Electoral coat of arms with the name and title of Christian I is used as an ornament on the inside of the lid. The knob of the lid was added in the 18th century.

By *Valentin Geitner*, master 1580. Prior to 1590. Dresden hall mark; master's mark R. 1731. Height 54 cm.; Inv. No. IV, 187.

Centre:

"Columbine" Goblet. Inside is the high six-edged point, which the interior of any masterpiece of a goldsmith's work had to show when its maker applied for admission to mastership in Nuremberg;

but in this goblet the point is soldered on. On the outside are three masterly embossed figures of soldiers, probably after *Goltzius*.

By *Georg Mond*, master before 1599, died after 1623. Dresden hall mark; master's mark R. 1740. Height 70 cm.; Inv. No. IV, 185.

Right:

Welcome Goblet from the Grünthal Smelting-Works. It is crowned by the figure of a smelter painted in cold colours; he holds in his hand a shield with the coat of arms of the Saxon Electorate. On the body of the goblet are embossed scenes illustrating the process of smelting; they are influenced by the woodcuts of a "Book On Mining" by *Georg Agricola*. A legend engraved on the inside of the lid explains the scenes: *Wer wissen will und fraget | hier | woher doch dieser Becher | rühr | der wüsse das mit grosser Zahl | Granalien hier in | Grünthal | versaigert worden und | probirt | und ehr also daraus formirt Anno 1625.* (Whoever seeks to know and asks whence this goblet came, may he be informed that here in Grünthal a great many granulated metals have been smelted and assayed to form this goblet in the year 1625). Another inscription which surrounds the rim of the lip reads: *Der churf. sächs. Saigerhütt Grünthal Gerechtigkeit und Wielkomm 1625.* (Electoral Saxon Smelting-Works Grünthal, Justice and Welcome, 1625). Under the foot is a plate of silver alloy with an embossed representation of Bacchus and Venus. The goblet was handed over to the Green Vaults in 1873 by the Grünthal Copperworks.

By *David Winckler*, master 1617, died 1635. Hall mark of Freiberg in Saxony; master's mark R. 2093.

Height 67 cm.; Inv. No. IV, 17.

37 Detail of the "Columbine" Goblet by Georg Mond

38 Detail of the Welcome Goblet by David Winckler

39 Three small Double Goblets

Silver gilt.

Two Double Goblets (halfes pear-shaped). By *Urban Schneeweiss*, 1536–1600. Late sixteenth century; Dresden hall mark; master's mark R. 1726. Height of each goblet 15 cm.; Inv. Nos. IV, 68; IV, 164; IV, 303; IV, 304.

Double Goblet (halfes hemispherical). The rims are surrounded by a legend which reads: *Nun gruss dich Gott du edels tranck, frisch mir mein Lebern, sie ist kranck. Mit dein gesunden helsamen tropffen. Du kanst mir wol mein Trawern verstopffen. Selig sey der backer der umb dich backet. Selig sey der läser, der dich erzwacket. Gesegne dich Gott alles tranck ein Kron. Dich fand von erst ein alter man. Noe der in der Archen was. Da er dein süsse beer auflass. Dein süsser Geschmack in da betrog. Unter einen stock er sich da schmag.* (God be with you, you noble drink; refresh my liver for it is sick. With your health-giving and healing drops you can cure my sadness. Blessed be he who hoes the ground around you, blessed be he who gathers you. God bless you, crown of all drinks. It was an old man who first discovered you, Noah, who was in the ark; he picked you, sweet berry, but your sweet taste deceived him: he fashioned a rod for his own back).

By *Kaspar Bauch the Elder*, master 1541, died 1583. Mid-sixteenth century. Nuremberg hall mark; master's marks R. 3856, R. 3857.

Height of each goblet 14.5 cm.; Inv. Nos. IV, 71; IV, 165.

40 Basin with Hunting Scenes

Silver gilt.

Masterly embossed work; only the front parts of the bodies of the horses and the heads of the four putti on the rim are cast work and screwed on.

By *Elias Geyer*, master 1589, died 1634. Leipzig hall mark; mark "F" of the years 1611–13; master's mark R. 3032. Measurements: 76 × 57.5 cm.;

Inv. No. IV, 250.

41 Gryphon, Jade Goblet, Basilisk

Silver gilt, nautilus shells, plates of jade.

All three works are by *Elias Geyer*, master 1589 in Leipzig, died 1634; master's mark R. 3032.

Left:

Drinking Vessel in the shape of a Gryphon. Mentioned in the inventory of 1610 of the Cabinet of Curiosities.

Leipzig hall mark; mark "C" of the years 1608–1610. Height 38.4 cm.;

Inv. No. IV, 127.

Centre:

Three-sided Goblet, formed of three plates of jade. Mentioned in the inventory of 1640 of the Cabinet of Curiosities.

Leipzig hall mark; master's mark R. 3032. About 1605. Height 43.9 cm.; Inv. No. IV, 199.

Right:

Drinking Vessel shaped as a Basilisk. Mentioned in the inventory of 1610 of the Cabinet of Curiosities. Although there are no marks undoubtedly by *Geyer*.

Height 33 cm.; Inv. No. IV, 158.

On all these three works there are fragments of cold colour painting, probably by Court Jeweller *Johann Heinrich Köhler*, who in 1724 restored the vessels to make them fit for exhibition in the Green Vaults.

42 Four Drinking Vessels in the shape of Ostriches

Ostrich eggs, silver and silver gilt.

These four works, although without marks, should be ascribed to *Elias Geyer*, master 1589 in Leipzig, died 1634. They are mentioned in the inventory of 1610 of the Cabinet of Curiosities. Height 46 cm.; Inv. No. III, 115; Height 44.5 cm.; Inv. No. III, 128; Height 47 cm.; Inv. No. III, 227; Height 46 cm.;

Inv. No. III, 114.

43 Travelling Casket and some of its Contents

Mother of pearl, core of wood, silver gilt, velvet, black mastic.

The casket is of oriental origin, the mount by *Elias Geyer*, master 1589, died 1634 in Leipzig. Inside are shelves and drawers lined with velvet. The illustration shows only part of the contents; some of these are marked with the Nuremberg hall mark and the master's mark R. 4049 of *G. Schuelein*, master 1587.

Leipzig hall mark, master's mark R. 3032 of *Elias Geyer*. Acquired by the Cabinet of Curiosities in 1602. Height 26.8 cm.; without lions: width 38.5 cm.; depth 22.6 cm.; Inv. No. III, 247.

44 Five Drinking Vessels in the shape of Sea-Horses

Silver gilt and oriental nautilus shells.

Four of these vessels are not marked; only that with the inventory number IV, 6 shows the master's mark R. 3032 of *Elias Geyer*, master 1589, died 1634. This vessel is also marked with the Leipzig hall mark and the mark "I" for either the years 1591–1593 or 1614–1616. As two vessels in the shape of sea-horses are already mentioned in the inventory of 1610 of the Cabinet of Curiosities, this whole group may have formed part of *Geyer's* early work; there can be no doubt that all five vessels, worked in an identical manner, came from his workshop.

Height 18 cm.; Inv. No. IV, 289; Height 17.7 cm.; Inv. No. IV, 126; Height 22 cm.; Inv. No. IV, 295; Height 17.8 cm.; Inv. No. IV, 4; Height 18.9 cm.;
Inv. No. IV, 6.

45 Basin, decorated with Mother of Pearl, and Jug

Mother of pearl, core of wood, black mastic, silver gilt.

The basin is of oriental origin; its mount in silver gilt and the jug are by *Elias Geyer*, master 1589, died 1634. The jug is made of pieces in solid cast work in silver gilt; a Renaissance work was used as model for it. At that time the Renaissance style also influenced the architecture of Saxony.

Jug: Leipzig hall mark; mark "F" for the years 1611–13; master's mark R. 3032. Height 35 cm.;
Inv. No. IV, 189.

Basin: Leipzig hall mark; master's mark R. 3032. Diameter 60.1 cm.; Inv. No. IV, 287.

46 Basin, decorated with Mother of Pearl, and Jug with Dragon

Small plates and shells of mother of pearl, core of wood, silver, parcel gilt.

The basin is of oriental origin. On its reverse side – below the mount – is a decoration in lacquer, showing hunting animals amidst tendrils on a salmon-pink background. The work on the jug was evidently influenced by *Christoph Jamnitzer*. The jug is filled through an opening below the ring around the neck; the lizards in the centre-panel of the basin are cast from nature. The basin and jug form a set.

By *Nicolaus Schmidt*, master 1582, died 1609. About 1600.

Basin: Nuremberg hall mark; Diameter 56 cm.; Inv. No. IV, 248.

Jug: Nuremberg hall mark; master's mark R. 4030. Height 41 cm.; Inv. No. IV, 157.

47 Three Goblets made of Nautilus Shells

Polished nautilus shells, silver gilt, gems.

Left:

Small Nautilus Goblet, supported by a tree trunk, which a kneeling peasant is trying to cut down. An interwoven fence surrounds a meadow painted in enamel. The straps are adorned with turquoises, garnets and rubies. On top is a grotesque mask and on it a monkey. The companion piece of this goblet was stolen in 1907.

There are no marks. South-German (Nuremberg?); about 1570. Height 17.8 cm.; Inv. No. III, 177.

Centre:

Nautilus Goblet on the Claw of an Eagle. The style of the foot is influenced by North-Italian bronze works. The claw, a very successful cast from nature, is akin to works by *Riccio*, the knob to those by *Vittoria*, while the bands and the scrollwork-grotesque follow Flemish models. The shell is a replacement of a broken original.

There are no marks; probably South-German; about 1580–1590.

Height 31 cm.;

Inv. No. III, 197.

Right:

Small Nautilus Goblet. The knob is decorated with half-length female figures in the style of the plaques by *Flötner*, sculptor and author of a book on art, published 1549.

By *Paulus Dulner*, master 1552, died 1596. About 1560–1570. Nuremberg hall mark; master's mark R. 3912. Height 18 cm.;

Inv. No. III, 181.

48 Five Drinking Vessels in the shape of Birds

Nautilus shells, silver gilt.

Above:

Cock. A Chinese (?) pattern is engraved into the shell.

By *Samuel Becker*, who can be traced from 1565 to 1601. Brunswick hall mark; master's mark R. 1311. Height 32 cm.; Inv. No. III, 153. (See W. Scheffler, *Goldschmiede Niedersachsens*, 1965, vol. 1, pp. 50/51, No. 58.)

Pelican feeding its young. At the foot four emeralds; below the pedestal the coat of arms of the town of Zwickau and the date 1609. The feet are cast from nature.

By *Christof Kunad*, master 1603. Nuremberg hall mark; master's mark R. 3867. Height 41 cm.;

Inv. No. III, 145.

Below:

Peacock. The head and tail are lacquered. The painting and two of the clasps were restored in 1724 by the Court Jeweller *Johann Heinrich Köhler* to make the goblet fit for exhibition in the Green Vaults. In the course of restoration after 1925 a new piece was soldered onto the tail at the point where it joins the body. (See J. L. Sponsel, *Das Grüne Gewölbe*, 1925, vol. I, plate 36.)

Perhaps by *Paulus Widmann*, master 1591 or 1592, died 1610. Nuremberg hall mark; master's mark R. 4061. Height 38 cm.;

Inv. No. III, 200.

Hen and Cock. Various Chinese (?) designs are engraved onto the shells. The legs are cast from nature.

By *Friedrich Hillebrand*, master 1580; died 1608. Nuremberg hall mark; master's mark R. 4017. Height 29 cm.; Inv. No. III, 193; Height 30 cm.;

Inv. No. III, 156.

49 Drinking Vessel in the shape of a Swan

Nautilus shell and silver, most of it gilded.

The opening is under the wings which can be lifted off. The legs up to the middle joint are cast from nature.

By *Friedrich Hillebrand*, master 1580, died 1608. Nuremberg hall mark; master's mark R. 4017. Height 39.5 cm.;

Inv. No. III, 143.

50 Three Nautilus Goblets

Shells polished or with designs in relief, silver gilt.

Left:

Nautilus Goblet with Chinese (?) scenes engraved into it. The cup is carried by a putto riding a dragon.

By *Hinrich Lambrecht* I, master 1599, died 1628. About 1620. Hamburg hall mark; master's mark R. 2380. Height 25.5 cm.; Inv. No. III, 186. (See W. Scheffler, *Goldschmiede Niedersachsens*, 1965, vol. I, pp. 413/414.)

Centre:

Nautilus Goblet, the Cup supported by Hercules, kneeling and carrying the terrestrial globe.

By *Friedrich Hillebrand*, master 1580, died 1608. About 1600. Nuremberg hall mark; master's mark R. 4017. Height 35.5 cm.;

Inv. No. III, 147.

Right:

Nautilus Goblet, supported on figure of a Triton.

By *Bartel Jamnitzer*, master 1575, died 1596. Nuremberg hall mark; master's mark R. 3836. Height 35.5 cm.; Inv. No. III, 262.

51 Three Drinking Vessels in the shape of Sailing Ships

Nautilus shells, silver gilt.

Left and Right:

Two Single-Masted Ships, each carried by a Triton resembling closely the Triton of the nautilus goblet by *Bartel Jamnitzer* (see No. 50).

By *Samuel Lormann*, early seventeenth century. Height 67 and 64.5 cm. respectively. Left: master's mark R. 4676; Height 67 cm.; Inv. No. III, 194. Right: hall mark of Torgau; Height 64.5 cm.; master's mark R. 4676; Inv. No. III, 191.

Centre:

Three-Masted Ship, carried by the figure of a kneeling Neptune. The figures of some of the crew seem to have been replaced in the eighteenth century.

By *Jörg Ruel*, master 1598, died 1625. Nuremberg hall mark; master's mark R. 4086. Height 59.5 cm.; Inv. No. III, 152.

52 A Parrot and a Partridge as Drinking Vessels, and a Flask with a Chain Handle

Mother of pearl, silver gilt, rubies, emeralds.

The *Parrot* is decorated with rubies, the stand with emeralds. The feathers of the tail were added in 1724 by the Court Jeweller *Johann Heinrich Köhler*.

By a Nuremberg master; the vessel is similar to works by *Friedrich Hillebrand*, though of inferior quality. About 1600. Nuremberg hall mark; master's mark of unknown master. Height 32.5 cm.; Inv. No. III, 151.

The *Partridge* is decorated with emeralds; particularly fine work. Identical drinking vessels in Leningrad and formerly in Gotha.

By *Friedrich Hillebrand*, master 1580, died 1608. Nuremberg hall mark; master's mark R. 4017. Height 27 cm.;

Inv. No. III, 150.

Flask with a Chain Handle, decorated with emeralds.
By *Jörg Ruel,* master 1598, died 1625. Nuremberg hall mark; master's mark R. 4086. Height 27.5 cm.; Inv. No. III, 192.

53 Two "Jungfrauenpokale", Goblets with Maidens as Supporting Figures

Silver, most of it gilded, nautilus shells.

Goblets like these were used at weddings; both cups were filled at the same time; the bridegroom had to show his skill in drinking from the larger cup formed by the maiden's skirt without spilling the wine from the smaller one. Afterwards the bride drank from the smaller cup tilting it towards herself with her lips.

Left:

Jungfrauenpokal; the nautilus is damaged.

By *Meinrad Bauch the Elder,* master 1575, died 1623. Late sixteenth century; Nuremberg hall mark; master's mark R. 3993. Height 27.5 cm.; Inv. No. III, 190.

Right:

Jungfrauenpokal, an outstanding work by *Friedrich Hillebrand,* master 1580, died 1608. The Court Jeweller *Johann Heinrich Köhler* restored the goblet in 1724 before it was taken to the Green Vaults for exhibition. He also made the clasp for the intersection of the straps below the nautilus.
About 1600. Nuremberg hall mark; master's mark R. 4017. Height 43 cm.; Inv. No. III, 184.

54 Drinking Vessel representing Daphne, and Ornate Jug

Silver, most of it gilded, corals.

Daphne; her skin is silver and her garment gilt. The upper part of her body can be lifted off at the waist. Originally laurel leaves in silver, probably painted green, were fixed to the coral branches. The vessel is almost identical with the Daphne by *Wenzel Jamnitzer.*

By *Abraham Jamnitzer,* master 1579, died about 1600. Nuremberg hall mark; master's mark R. 3838. Height 68 cm.; Inv. No. IV, 260.

Ornate Jug known as Dragon Jug. The jug is crowned by the figure of Minerva. Its body is embossed with heart-shaped bosses. Into four of these are chased in the most delicate work pictures of the seasons. In the inventory of the Silver Room of 1723 a basin is mentioned as belonging to the jug, but it was probably melted down in the eighteenth century.

By *Christoph Jamnitzer,* master 1592, died 1618. Early seventeenth century; Nuremberg hall mark; master's mark R. 3839. Height 46 cm.; Inv. No. IV, 239.

55 Two Drinking Vessels representing Actaeon and a Leaping Stag

Silver gilt and corals.

Actaeon, accompanied by two dogs.

By *Jeremias Ritter,* master 1605, died 1646. Nuremberg hall mark; master's mark R. 3882. Height 50 cm.; Inv. No. IV, 261.

Leaping Stag, supported on the trunk of a tree. It is being attacked by a small dog. A man with an axe stands in the fork of the branches of the tree.

By *Andreas Rosa,* master 1599. Early seventeenth century; Nuremberg hall mark; master's mark R. 4099. Height 42 cm.;
Inv. No. IV, 119.

56 Drinking Vessel representing St. George

Silver gilt.

This is a joke-tankard. The heads of the knight, of the horse and of the dragon can be lifted off; the bodies of all three figures form interconnecting vessels. The problem is how to drink from any one of the figures, without letting the liquor pour out of the others. It can be solved if the figure of the knight is lifted off his horse, which is quite easy, as it is only pegged onto it. The figures are cast in silver gilt. The monogram "FAC" and the Elector's hat are engraved into the knight's shield; the letters are the initials of Augustus the Strong, used by him after he became Elector in 1694 and before he was crowned King of Poland in 1697.

By *Hans Keller*, master 1582, died 1609. About 1600. Nuremberg hall mark; master's mark R. 4032. Height 52 cm.; Inv. No. IV, 124.

57 Two Astronomical Time-Pieces

Gilded bronze.

The Smaller Clock is painted white, green, blue and red; there are eight dials; on top there was formerly a figure of Fortuna, which, however, was lost in the Second World War.

By *Jeremias Metzker* of Augsburg, about 1560. Height 27.3 cm.; Inv. No. IV, 1.

The Larger Clock with five dials. There are etched Moresque ornaments and inscriptions, explaining the functions of the dials; added to the inscriptions is the master's signature: *Andreas Schelborn 1571. z Schnebergk in Meisen.* Height 39 cm.; Inv. No. IV, 3.

58 Jewellery Chest of Ebony

Ebony, gold, enamel.

In the niches and on the curved lid are female figures representing the virtues. A reclining putto with an hour glass and a skull holds a tablet inscribed *memento mori*. The figures as well as all the ornaments and the enamelling are work of the finest quality. There is a similarity to the pendants known as "Caritas" and "David and Goliath", which are also in the Green Vaults.

Probably German, late sixteenth century. Measurements: 32×32×22 cm.; Inv. No. V, 596.

59 Calvary

Silver gilt, wood, shells of pearl-oyster, irregular pearls, emeralds, turquoises, garnets.

On the hill made of pearls are twigs and small animals cast in silver from nature. In the grotto stands a heron; Christ's garment is coloured red. The Cross is made of so-called king's wood or iron wood, a particularly hard wood from the tropics. The date 1577 is painted in gold on the foot of the Cross. Six reliefs showing Christ's Passion decorate the pedestal, in the frontal part of which are two drawers.

By *Elias Lencker*, master 1562, died 1591. Nuremberg hall mark; master's mark R. 3951. Measurements: 67×31×19.3 cm.; Inv. No. III, 187.

60 Sewing Chest

Silver, parcel gilt, shells, gems, velvet, core of wood.

In the glass-covered niches stand the figures of ten virtues. A row of drawers is fixed into the back of the interior of the chest. Inside as well as outside it is richly decorated with gems and with pieces of velvet in various shades. Most of the silver ornaments are prefabricated pressed or cast pieces. Although this is interesting from the point of view of technique, it is of little value as a work of art. According to the inventory of 1640 of the Cabinet of Curiosities this *Kästli oder Näblädlein* (small chest or sewing chest) was presented by the wife of the Elector of Brandenburg to Elector Christian I in 1590.

Probably from a workshop in Nuremberg, late sixteenth century. Measurements: 42×49×36 cm.; Inv. No. IV, 145.

61 Jewellery Chest

Silver, gilded copper and brass.

The chest is made of heavy cast plates, covered outside and inside with beautifully etched Moresques. There are embossed reliefs of the Passion of Christ, and on the lid a cast relief of the Resurrection. The ornamental bands are cast in silver. There are similar chests in Lisbon, Volterra, Innsbruck, the Rothschild Collection and there was also formerly one at Munich. Their style suggests the circle around *Jamnitzer* in Nuremberg.

The chest has been ascribed to *Jacob Mores the Elder* from Hamburg, because of a drawing by him, which to a great extent corresponds with it. *Mores* became a master in 1579, and died in 1609; his master's mark was R.2376. It is, however, possible that – because of their material – these chests were not made in a goldsmith's workshop, but in that of a South-German worker in brass. About 1580. Measurements: 41 × 37 × 28 cm.; Inv. No. IV, 33.

62 Three Spoons of Gold

Gold, enamel, gems, sardonyx.

Left:

Spoon; its bowl is in oriental sardonyx, the handle covered with flowers in translucent and opaque enamel and decorated with the letter "K", surmounted by a crown. It was a present from the Princess of Teschen to Augustus the Strong.

German, late seventeenth century. Length 16 cm.; Inv. No. V, 2 yy.

Centre:

Cutlery Set; the fork and spoon fit together and are set with brilliants and rubies. Originally there was also a toothpick with the kneeling figure of a princess fixed on to the end of its handle; this was later on replaced by the figure of a dancing harlequin in gold-enamel by *Johann Melchior Dinglinger,* which in its turn was removed in 1929 and put on a stand of its own. The set was a present from the "Kronmarschallin" Mnisczek in Warsaw to Augustus the Strong at his birthday in 1724.

Probably Nuremberg work, resembling that of *Friedrich Hillebrand.* About 1600. Length 23 cm.; Inv. No. VI, 7 m.

Right:

Spoon, the bowl in oriental sardonyx, the handle decorated with rubies, pearls and a brilliant. German, late sixteenth century. Length 11.7 cm.; Inv. No. V, 2 zz.

63 Seven Chains of Gold

Gold, enamel, lapis lazuli.

From Left to Right:

Girdle Chain, consisting of thirty-four round beads of lapis lazuli and thirty-four heart-shaped beads of gold, showing the letter "A" in relief on both sides. The chain came from the treasury of Anna, 1548–1585, wife of Elector Augustus.

German, third quarter of sixteenth century. Inv. No. VIII, 279.

Girdle Chain, formed of fifty-eight beads in enamelled gold.

German, Spanish in style; third quarter of sixteenth century. Inv. No. VIII, 272.

Girdle Chain, formed of forty-seven hollow almond-shaped beads in openwork of gold and enamel.

German, late sixteenth century. Inv. No. VIII, 270.

Necklace, consisting of thirty-eight enamelled links, shaped like branches of foliage.

German, about 1600. Inv. No. VIII, 259.

Girdle Chain, formed of forty-seven enamelled beads and a pear-shaped pendant. All the beads are decorated with the interlaced "AA". The chain came from the treasury of Anna, 1548–1585, wife of Elector Augustus.

German, third quarter of sixteenth century. Inv. No. VIII, 277.

Chain in the shape of an Anchor Chain; it consists of one hundred and thirty-seven links, some straight, some twisted.

Sixteenth century. Inv. No. VIII, 275.

Chain to be worn as Belt, consisting of twenty-five hollow, almond-shaped beads, decorated with enamel, and an equally hollow, egg-shaped pendant. German, about 1600. Inv. No. VIII, 273.

64 Mirror with Ornate Frame in the shape of a Tomb

Plate-glass, silver, most of it gilded, rock crystal, amethysts, églomisé painting.

The influence of Dutch art is discernible in the frame. The relief figures are cast in silver, hollow and open at the back. The decoration represents an allegory of the everlasting Holy Roman Empire, based on the dream of Nebuchadnezzar, expounded by Daniel the Prophet. The men on horseback above the mirror represent Babylon and Persia, the warriors at its sides Greece and Rome as the Fourth and Last Empire. The figure crowning the mirror is Nebuchadnezzar, immediately below him is an escutcheon with the imperial eagle behind a crucifix. On the removable cover of the mirror there is a design of the globe with the lamenting Spirit of Time. A quotation from Galen is painted in églomisé technique on the reverse side of the cover; it is damaged, however, and difficult to read; it ends with the words: *Hilf uns, du heilige Dreifaltigkeit, Amen. 1592*. (Help us, holy Trinity, Amen. 1592.) This was the motto of Sophia, wife of Elector Christian I. The incised monogram "LM" shows that the mirror is the work of *Luleff Meier*, master at Lüneburg, 1592. According to the inventory of the Cabinet of Curiosities of 1610 the mirror was bought from a man in Lüneburg, probably from the master himself.

Measurement: 115 × 85 cm.; Inv. No. IV, 110.

65 Detail of the Ornate Frame of the Mirror

Allegories of *fides, caritas, pax, respublica, prudentia*, and *lex* (from left to right). The figure in the centre cannot be identified with certainty.

66 Five Pendants

Gold, gems, enamel.

From Top to Bottom:

Coat of Arms of the Electorate of Saxony. Twenty-eight rubies, four emeralds, seventy-seven diamonds.

Probably Saxon, by *Gabriel Gipfel*, 1610/1611. Measurements: 12.2 × 7.3 cm.; Inv. No. VIII, 271.

Monogram AA.

Twelve rubies, two emeralds, twenty diamonds.

The letters "AA" are the monogram of Elector Augustus (1553–1586), and his wife Anna.

German, 1550–1570. Measurements: 6.7 × 6.5 cm.; Inv. No. VIII, 286.

Rosette.

Three rubies, three emeralds, twelve diamonds.

First half of sixteenth century. Measurements: 5.2 × 4.4 cm.; Inv. No. VIII, 298.

St. George.

Six rubies, one emerald, ten diamonds, seven pearls.

Second half of sixteenth century. Measurements: 8.3 × 5.1 cm.; Inv. No. VIII, 265.

Judgement of Paris.

Nine rubies, twenty-seven diamonds.

German, about 1600. Measurements: 9.1 × 6.7 cm.;

Inv. No. VIII, 290.

67 Ten Pendants

Gold, enamel, gems.

From Top to Bottom:

Warrior with Scimitar.

Eighteen diamonds. Head of gold, enamelled in white. This figure forms the centre of a pendant. There is a comparable work on a small case dated 1533 in Leningrad.

Early sixteenth century. Length from right foot to right hand 4.4 cm.; Inv. No. VI, 7 e.

Warrior with Sword.

Twenty-one diamonds. The warrior's face is cut in mother of pearl. This figure forms the centre of a pendant. There is a comparable work on a small case dated 1533 in Leningrad.

Early sixteenth century. Length from left foot to right hand 5 cm.; Inv. No. VI, 7 d.

Siren.

Three rubies, forty-eight diamonds.

Late sixteenth century. Measurements: 8.4 × 6.7 cm.; Inv. No. VIII, 292.

Monogram A.

Twelve diamonds.

The letter "A" is the monogram either of Elector Augustus, who reigned from 1553 to 1586, or of his wife Anna (1548–1585).

Probably French, about 1560. Measurements: 6.6 × 5 cm.; Inv. No. VIII, 301.

Monogram IGH.

Twenty rubies, thirty-nine diamonds. The letters "IGH" are the monogram of Duke John George I, Elector of Saxony (1611–1656).

German, early seventeenth century. Measurements: 8.6 × 5.9 cm.; Inv. No. VIII, 297.

Stag with Woman playing the Lute.
Sixteen rubies, ten diamonds, one pearl.
German, late sixteenth century. Measurements: 5 × 4.3 cm.; Inv. No. VI, 7 h.
David and Goliath.
Eighteen rubies, forty-seven diamonds.
German, late sixteenth century. Measurements: 9.9 × 6.8 cm.; Inv. No. VIII, 294.
Head of Warrior.
One ruby, three diamonds, mother of pearl.
German, late sixteenth century. Height 4.9 cm.; Inv. No. VI, 81 h.
Pikeman.
Eight rubies, two diamonds. On his back is the motto: *Pro patria*, after *Goltzius*, Dutch
painter and engraver.
German, about 1590. Height 6.6 cm.; Inv. No. VI, 81 m.
Musketeer.
Twenty-six rubies, one diamond.
German, about 1590; after *Goltzius*, Dutch painter and engraver. Height 6.2 cm.; Inv. No. VI,
81 l.

68 Two Figures carrying Wine-Tubs

Wood and silver.
Although both figures were carved at approximately the same time and probably at the same
place, they did not originally form a pair. Both are very well carved. On the tub of the vintager
is the Strassbourg hall mark and the master's mark R.6983 of *Paul Ölinger* who became master in
1612. The mount of the figure of the female vintager is by another hand; it resembles the mount
of a smaller couple with tubs of inferior quality, but evidently from the same circle of sculptors;
this too is in the Green Vaults (Inv. Nos. VII, 6 and 7). In the eyes of the female vintager described here and in those of the smaller couple the pupils are made with pins in silver stuck into
the eye-balls.
Probably from Alsace, perhaps Strassbourg; early seventeenth century. Height 24.5 cm.; Inv. No.
VII, 4; Height 23 cm.; Inv. No. VII, 5.

69 Three small Caskets, covered with Mother of Pearl

Silver gilt, mother of pearl, rock crystal, chrysolites, amethysts.
All three caskets are of oriental origin. Their cores are of wood, mounted in silver gilt and painted
salmon-pink; inside they are lined with woven textile of various colours.
Left:
Casket, standing on the Figures of Four Sirens.
Mount by *Nicolaus Schmidt*, master 1582, died 1609. Nuremberg hall mark; master's mark
R. 4030. Measurements: 17 × 27 × 17.5 cm.; Inv. No. III, 55.
Centre:
Casket, standing on Four Snails, decorated with chrysolites and amethysts. Mount by *Nicolaus
Schmidt*, master 1582, died 1609.
Nuremberg hall mark; master's mark R. 4030. Measurements: 23 × 36 × 22.5 cm.; Inv. No. III,
244.

Right:

Small Pharmacist's Casket, standing on four knobs of rock crystal. Inside are nine glass bottles, six small ivory boxes, four other boxes, two cups, and one spatula in gilded silver. There is no mark on the casket, but it too is probably from Nuremberg, late sixteenth century. Measurements: 19 × 28.5 × 18 cm.; Inv. No. III, 243.

70 Disk with Coat of Arms, Mirror, Pendants, Rings

Above, left:

Round Disk in Verre Églomisé with the coat of arms of the Electorate of Saxony and an inscription reading: *Augustus Herzog zu Sachsen, des Heiligen Römischen Reiches Ertzmarschall und Chur Fürst Landgraf in Duringen, Marg Graf zu Meissen und Burg Graf zu Magdeburgk Anno 1586* (Augustus, Duke of Saxony, Arch-Marshall and Elector of the Holy Roman Empire, Landgrave of Thuringia, Margrave of Meissen and Burghgrave of Magdeburg A.D. 1586). The mount is of enamelled gold, on its reverse side are remnants of a portrait on copper of the Elector.

Mount by *Valentin Geitner*, master in Dresden 1580, master's mark R.1731. He was paid for his work in 1588. Diameter 12.5 cm.; Inv. No. V, 614.

Above, right:

Disk with Representation of Baptism of Christ. The disk is of enamelled silver in the style of the Nuremberg master *Elias Lencker*, late sixteenth century.

Diameter 11 cm.; Inv. No. III, 38.

Centre, left:

Pendant with Portrait of Elector Christian II. Gold, pearls, enamel. A legend on the pendant reads: *initium sapientiae timor domini.* The portrait-medallion is by *Tobias Wolf* of Dresden. On the part of the arm shown in the medallion is the monogram of the master and the date 1601.

Mount perhaps by *Gabriel Gipfel.* Acquired 1892.

Measurements of the medallion: 2.9 × 2.3 cm.; Inv. No. VIII, 390.

Centre, middle:

Lozenge-shaped Mirror, reverse side gold and enamel; the central panel shows the Three Wise Men. Under the hinged panel is a portrait, painted in oil on silver, of Sophia, the widow of Elector Christian I, in her old age; she died in 1622.

Probably German, early seventeenth century. Measurements: 18 × 15 cm.; Inv. No. VI, 64.

Centre, right:

Pendant with Portrait of Sophia, wife of Elector Christian I. Gold and enamel. Inscription on the reverse side: *Hilf Du Heilige Dreifaltigkeit. Anno 1589* (Help, holy Trinity, A.D. 1589).

By *Tobias Wolf* of Dresden; the mount perhaps by *Gabriel Gipfel.* Acquired 1888. Diameter of medallion: 3.2 cm.; Inv. No. VIII, 421.

Below from Left to Right:

Ring of Gold with Octagonal Sapphire. Mounted in black enamel. Said to have been a present from Elector John Frederic (1532–1547) to Ritter Thilo von Trotha, when the latter made him a prisoner of war in the battle of Mühlberg in 1547.

Inv. No. VIII, 96.

Ring of Gold with Cone-shaped Turquoise. Mount enamelled in black and decorated with six table-cut brilliants.

Early seventeenth century; Inv. No. VIII, 75.

Ring of Gold with an Aureus of Emperor Septimius Severus, set à jour. The ring was found near Mühlberg and may therefore have been lost in the battle of 1547.

Mount probably German, mid-sixteenth century; acquired 1890. Inv. No. VIII, 386.

Ring of Gold with Pyramidal Diamond. On the enamelled mount are four triangular diamonds and ten table-cut brilliants.

Third quarter of sixteenth century. Inv. No. VIII, 56.

Ring of Gold with Table-Cut Piece of Rock Crystal.

Probably by *Abraham Schwedler* of Dresden. Second quarter of seventeenth century. Inv. No. VIII, 387.

71 Two Jugs of Amber

Amber, gold, diamonds, pearls, enamel.

Left:

Small Jug with Lid; mounted in gold and enamel.

Königsberg, about 1610. Height 13.4 cm.; Inv. No. III, 79.

Right:

Jug with Lid; the jug's body is decorated with the figures of eight Greek gods. The mount is of gold and enamel; the lid is decorated with diamonds.

Style of *Schreiber's* workshop in Königsberg, about 1620. Height 20.5 cm.; Inv. No. III, 78.

72 Wheelbarrow-Group

Silver gilt.

The devil in a barrel pushes along a drunkard. *Peter Flötner* and an artist known only by his monogram *bg*, second half of the 15th century, have a similar motif (see E.F. Bange, Ill. 6). Under the barrel is a bell; on top the following legend: *Die arbeit ist mir vil zu schwer | Mein Bachus der is selten ler.* On the devil's apron are the words: *Comedite et bibite Post mortem nulla voluptas.* There is a further inscription on the wheelbarrow, reading: *Ich bin einn man Gross unnd dickh | ich het meinn tag vil grosses glückh | fressen und trinken dz stud mir zu | tag und nacht het ich keinn rub | mit schone weibern het grossen lust | macht das ich jetzt farenn mues | ich far daher mit heeres krafft | kum her Du edler rebenn safft | unnd alle gute gesellschafft. Der Got Bachus binn ich genant | bei mir ist scheisse speien kein schnd | wellcher das besst zu thun vermag | der ist ein engel am jüngsten tag | Darumb las ime ein jedweder sein | Mein epicurisch leben bevolhē seī | So früe inn morgēs dürstē mag | findt er mich willig nacht uñ tag.* One more inscription is below the wheelbarrow: *Die glocken hat ein fremden thon | Der sie vil leit, mus an de wende gan.*

By *Christoph Lindenberger*, master 1546, died 1580. Mid-sixteenth century; Nuremberg hall mark; master's mark R. 3878. Height 19 cm.; Inv. No. IV, 337.

73 Five Goblets made of Ostrich Eggs

Ostrich eggs, silver gilt, oil paint.

From Left to Right:

Goblet with Supporting Figure of a Kneeling Red Indian. The lid is crowned by a figure of Cupid, perhaps a later addition. On the ring around the foot are two incomplete marks, which cannot be identified.

Probably German, early seventeenth century. Height 42.4 cm.; Inv. No. III, 116.

Goblet with Staff-Like Shaft surrounded by Tendrils. The egg is damaged. The knob on the lid was added in 1724 by the Court Jeweller *Johann Heinrich Köhler.* On the lining of the lid are the Nuremberg hall mark and the master's mark R. 4030 of *Nicolaus Schmidt,* who became a master in 1582 and died in 1609. It is, however, uncertain whether this lid originally belonged to the goblet. Probably South-German, about 1600. Height 37.3 cm.; Inv. No. III. 226.

Goblet with Supporting Figure of a Kneeling Youth. On the lid is a satyr carrying a dragon and on the latter a man thrusting his lance into the dragon's mouth. There are traces of painting on this group, and on the egg itself there are three scenes painted in oil; the Annunciation, the Adoration of the Shepherds and the Circumcision of Christ.

There is no mark. German, early seventeenth century. Height 47.4 cm.; Inv. No. III, 110.

Goblet with Figure of a Warrior on the Lid. The warrior holds a shield. The coats of arms of Brandenburg and of the Dukes of Saxony are riveted onto the egg just below the rim of the lip; a third coat of arms is missing. It is obvious that the lid did not originally belong to this goblet. There is a hall mark on it, showing a city gate and a master's mark "HN", perhaps R. 9482. Both, goblet and lid, date from about 1600. Height 41.5 cm.; Inv. No. III, 223.

Goblet carried on a Branch by a Peasant. The goblet was a present given in 1649 to Elector John George I by his wife Magdalene Sybil. The peasant is superbly modelled, showing traces of painting. On the lid are a figure of Athena of middling quality, acanthus leaves and scrollwork with masks embossed in high-relief. The style of the lid is different from that of the goblet. Late sixteenth century. There is no mark. German, perhaps by *Elias Geyer* of Leipzig or *Nicolaus Schmidt* of Nuremberg? Height 45.5 cm.; Inv. No. III, 117.

74 Two Vessels of Rock Crystal

Mounts of silver gilt, decorated with enamel and gems.

Tall Jug of rock crystal with silver-gilt lid, shaped like the head of a dragon. The vessel came from the Court workshop in Prague; it is reminiscent of the style of *Dionysio Miseroni,* mid-seventeenth century. The mount is probably German, second half of seventeenth century.
Height 42 cm.; Inv. No. V, 183.

Tall Goblet of rock crystal with a chiselled grotesque mask on the back.
Probably from Prague, late seventeenth century. Height 34 cm.; Inv. No. V, 250.

75 Miner's Outfit for John George II.

Silver, parcel gilt, enamel, garnets, rock crystal, opals, amethysts, smoky topaz, iron, leather.
This ceremonial outfit for the Miners' Festival made for the Elector was intended to symbolize the importance of mining for Saxony. There are several inscriptions on the shaft of the axe: *Die Steine so auf disen Berghabit vorhanden / sind durch Gottes Segen gefunden in disen Landen* (Through God's mercy the stones on these garments were found in this country). On the base of the shaft: *Das Silber zu disen Werck gab durch Gottes Segen der St. Daniel zum Schneberg 1676 SK fecit* (God blessed the mine of St. Daniel at Schneeberg to produce the silver for this work 1676 SK fecit). St. Daniel was the name of the silver-mine at Schneeberg. Like these and similar legends, the enamel paintings too refer to mining and miners (See detailed description in *Der Bergmannsschmuck Johann Georg II von Sachsen,* edited and introduced by H. Winkelmann, Bochum 1962). A further signature, apart from that mentioned above, appears on the large enamel plate on the pouch: *Freib S. Klem. Aetatis suae 66 Ao.1677.*

By the Freiberg goldsmith *Samuel Klemm*, master 1644, died 1678; master's mark R.2097. About 1675–1677. Length of sword from pommel to point of scabbard 80 cm.; Inv. Nos. VIII, 317–324.

76 Four Goblets of Ivory and Three Curiosities of Ivory

Ivory.

From Left to Right:

Two Goblets Combined in One, signed "EL 1589". Inside the cubes and the sphere are freely-moving balls.

Height 61 cm.; Inv. No. II, 415.

Two Goblets Combined in One, signed "EL 1590". The coat of arms of the Saxon Electorate and the name of Christian I are painted on glass in églomisé technique inside the lid of the larger goblet.

By *Egidius Lobenigk* from Cologne, Court Turner in Dresden from 1584 until his death sometime before 10th April 1595.

Height 53 cm.; Inv. No. II, 282.

Four Goblets combined in One. The point is broken off. Signed "GW 1588". Height 70 cm.; Inv. No. II, 161.

Double Goblet, signed "GW", signature of *Georg Wecker* from Munich, Court Turner in Dresden from 1578 onwards. The goblet, made in 1611, was the last work signed by him now in the possession of the Green Vaults.

Height 28 cm.; Inv. No. II, 380. Height 27 cm.; Inv. No. II, 381.

Column, signed with the letters "GF" and with a star and a heron. The point which originally passed through the upper ring is broken off.

By *Georg Friedel*, Court Turner in the Electorate of the Palatinate, first half of seventeenth century. The column came to the Cabinet of Curiosities in 1619.

Height 60 cm.; Inv. No. II, 298.

Curiosity, an object where the technical virtuosity outweighs any artistic value. The point is broken off. There is no master's mark. The "Curiosity" came to the Cabinet of Curiosities in 1619.

Height 58 cm.; Inv. No. II, 255.

Column, signed "EL 1591" by *Egidius Lobenigk*.

Height 70 cm.; Inv. No. II, 99.

77 Ivory Goblet and Concentric Pierced Sphere of Ivory

Ivory.

The Goblet is crowned by the figure of St. George fighting the dragon; legend on lid: *ceu drako devictus manibus gladioque Georgi, sic satanam fudit victor iesus humi*. A tree with an ithyphallic satyr forms the shaft. *Jacobus Zeller fecit et inv. 1613* is inscribed in relief under the base.

Height 51 cm.; Inv. No. II, 154.

Concentric Pierced Sphere; this sphere contains another in rich openwork with medallions of outstanding workmanship showing the portraits of Elector Christian II and his wife Edwiga – an amazing achievement in both technique and art. On top of the sphere is a boy sitting on a skull while he blows soap-bubbles, a vanitas-motif copied from *Goltzius*, Dutch painter and engraver; *Jacob Zeller 1611* is inscribed in relief under the base.

Jacob Zeller from Regensburg was Court Turner in Dresden from 1610 until his death in 1620.

Height 30.5 cm.; Inv. No. II, 296.

78 Venus with Mirror

Ivory sculpture, probably by *Melchior Barthel*, 1625–1672. Height 30.5 cm.; Inv. No. II, 335.

79 Frigate of Ivory

Ivory.

The rigging, nails and guns are of gold. On the hull are eight bands enumerating the rulers of Saxony from Widukind to the then reigning Elector John George I. On the large sail of the middle mast are the coats of arms of the Elector and his wife Magdalene Sybil of Brandenburg in masterly relief work. A Triton behind Neptune holds a tablet with the signature *Jacobus Zeller C. S. bestalter Kunstdresdler fecit et inventavit 1620* (bestalter Kunstdresdler = commissioned turner in ivory.) The frigate came to the Cabinet of Curiosities in 1620.

Measurements: 115 × 80 cm.; Inv. No. II, 107.

80 Bull being tamed by Two Men

Ivory sculpture on original pedestal of wood. Modelled after "Farnese Bull".

By *Melchior Barthel*, 1625–1672, who became Court Sculptor in Dresden in 1670. Measurements: 39.5 × 35 × 19 cm.; Inv. No. II, 47.

81 Two Tankards of Ivory

Ivory mounted in silver gilt.

Left:

Tankard with Relief of Women in Bathhouse.

German, early seventeenth century. Mount by *Martin Borisch*, master 1613, died 1649. Dresden hall mark; master's mark R.1749. Height 33.5 cm.; Inv. No. II, 22.

Right:

Tankard with Relief of a Bacchic Procession.

After *Georg Petel*; South-German, mid-seventeenth century. Mount by *Daniel Harnischter*, master 1651; Strassbourg hall mark; master's mark R. 6986. Height 27 cm.; Inv. No. II, 395.

82 Two Goblets in the shape of Globes

Silver, parcel gilt.

To the left Hercules carrying the terrestrial globe crowned by Jupiter's eagle with a bundle of lightning shafts, to the right St. Christopher carrying the celestial sphere crowned by the Christ Child administering the blessing. The spheres were exchanged at the end of the nineteenth century. They can be used as goblets, splitting into cup and lid at the line of the equator. The terrestrial sphere is signed *Johannes Schmidt sculpsit*. Its design is evidently based on one of the maps by *Hondius*; the most important discoveries are inscribed, the latest being that of the Straits of Cape Hoorne, 1616. In the embossed pedestals of the goblets are mechanisms with which to steer them across the table; probably the person in front of whom they came to a standstill had to empty them.

Augsburg hall mark; master's mark L, R. 547, which could not yet be allocated to any master; perhaps a member of the family of *Lencker*. Philipp Hainhofer saw the goblets in 1629 in the Cabinet of Curiosities.

Hercules: height 64 cm.; Inv. No. IV, 294; St. Christopher: height 64 cm.; Inv. No. IV, 290.

83 Detail of Plate 82: St. Christopher

For this figure and for that of Hercules, both cast in silver, the models were probably provided by professional sculptors. It has been proved that a small bronze by *Jacopo Sansovino*, which is in Moscow, was used as model for the Hercules (see H. R. Weihrauch, in the publication in honour of Theodor Müller in Munich, 1965). Still closer is the resemblance to a Florentine bronze of the sixteenth century, reproduced in the catalogue for the Spring Exhibition of Peel & Humphrey Ltd. in London in 1964. For the Christopher too some Italian model may have been used.

84 Jewellery Chest

Ebony and silver, parcel gilt.
A clock with two enamelled dials is set in the steeple-like central part of the chest. Inside are doors and drawers in rich architectural designs and decorated with reliefs in silver, with figures and ornaments.
By *Matthaeus Wallbaum*, master after 1588, died 1630 or 1632. Augsburg hall mark; master's mark R. 428. Early seventeenth century.
Measurements: 85.5 × 53.5 × 38.5 cm.; Inv. No. I, 34.

85 Domestic Altar

Silver and ebony.
One wing and the mandorla of the angel who crowns the altar were lost in the Second World War. The relief of the Resurrection on the tomb is signed with the letters "HKD08".
By *Hans Kellerthaler* of Dresden, 1608. *Kellerthaler* is mentioned as being a master from 1585 to 1637; his master's mark is R. 1732. The altar was a present from Elector Christian II to Duchess Magdalene Sybil, wife of Elector John George I, Christmas 1608.
Height 104 cm.; Inv. No. I, 18.

86 Three Vessels of Saxon Serpentine

Serpentine, mounts of silver gilt.
Left:
Barrel.
No mark on the mount; German, early seventeenth century. Length 18 cm.; Inv. No. V, 410.
Centre:
Canister with Lid and Two Ring-like Handles.
Mount by *Zacharias Schlosser the Younger*, apprentice 1640–1646; died 1676. Dresden hall mark; master's mark R. 1764. Acquired 1927. Height 24 cm.; Inv. No. 1927/6.
Right:
Jug with Arched Handle.
No mark on the mount; its style is akin to that of the barrel.
German, early seventeenth century.
Height without handle 18 cm.; Inv. No. V, 396.

87 Group of the Three Graces

Amber.

Attributed to the *Master of the Judgement of Paris* in Königsberg. North-East German, about 1670. Height 16 cm.; Inv. No. III, 64.

88 Bowl of Amber

Amber, mount in silver gilt.

In the panels of translucent amber are reliefs, some of them engraved and lined with silver foil, others sculptured in a wax-like material. One of the reliefs is the coat of arms of Brandenburg. According to the inventory of 1741, the bowl, which came from the estate of an Elector's widow, was "handed over" in 1687 – probably to the Cabinet of Curiosities. Most likely it had belonged to Magdalene Sybil of the familiy of the Margraves of Brandenburg, married to Elector John George I in 1607; she died in 1659.

A small jug (Inv. No. III, 79, Plate 71) probably belonged to this bowl. On the mount of the bowl is the master's mark "AM" not yet identified, perhaps it is that of a master from Königsberg; no hall marking was practised in the seventeenth century in the towns of North-East Germany. Königsberg, about 1610. Diameter 46 cm.; Inv. No. III, 76.

89 The Archangel Michael defeats Satan

Limewood.

An outstanding work. There is a likeness between this and the bronze group by *Hubert Gerhards* at the St. Michael's Church in Munich.

South-German, early seventeenth century. Height 61 cm.; Inv. No. I, 41.

90 Diana on a Centaur; a mechanical Contrivance

Silver, parcel gilt, rubies, emeralds, enamel, ebony, four clock works.

On the front of the pedestal is a clock with a striking apparatus and an enamelled dial. The contrivance can drive over the table on wheels, while two of the dogs on it jump and the third turns its head, the centaur shoots an arrow and he and Diana move their eyes.

Acquired in Prague in 1610 by Elector Christian II. A comparable piece by the same master is in Vienna.

Augsburg hall mark; not yet elucidated master's mark R. 544. Height 47 cm.; Inv. No. IV, 150.

91 Two Figures of Athena

Silver

Left:

Figure of Athena. The left hand originally held a spear. The figure is made of pieces of embossed silver, soldered together.

By *Abraham Drentwett*, mentioned 1649, died 1666. Augsburg hall mark; master's mark R. 597. Height without base 42 cm.; Inv. No. IV, 305.

Right:

Figure of Athena, like the previous one also made of pieces of embossed silver, soldered together.

By *Philipp Küsel*, who died in the year 1700. Late seventeenth century. Augsburg hall mark; master's mark R. 652. Height without base and spear 39 cm.; Inv. No. IV, 25.

92 Chequer-Board

Wood.

The cover of the board is decorated with marquetry inside and out; some of the pieces of wood are stained. A relief on the flap represents Hannibal at the battle of Zama. Signed: *Job: Georg: Fischer fecit Anno 1655*. A chequer-board dated 1661 by the same master from Eger, and with the same design, is now in Berlin.

Measurements: 54.5 × 54.5 × 13 cm.; Inv. No. VII, 250.

93 Charles II of England as St. George defeats the Dragon of the Revolution

Iron.

The seven-headed monster excretes the head of Oliver Cromwell. The sword of St. George was lost in the Second World War. On the pedestal are two cartouches of iron, the one in front is inscribed: *Carol.II.M.Brit.Rex.Vitia.Sub. Imag.D.Georgi. Vincens* (Carolus II Magnae Brittaniae Rex, vitia, sub imagine Divi Georgii, vincens). On the reverse side is a portrait of Charles I. By *Gottfried Christian Leygebe* of Nuremberg after 1660, the year after the entry of Charles II into London. Bought for six hundred Thaler by Frederic William I, Elector of Brandenburg, and presented by him to the Elector John George II. It came to the Cabinet of Curiosities in 1667. Joachim von Sandrart gives a detailed description of it in the *Teutsche Academie*, published by him in Nuremberg 1679, vol.2, book 3, p. 86. He says that the master sculptured the group by carving it with a hammer and a graving tool out of a block of iron weighing sixty-seven pounds. Similar but less weighty groups by *Leygebe* are in Copenhagen and in Berlin. In 1960 the restorer of the Historical Museum in Dresden, Kurt Andrich, discovered, as he was cleaning the group, that it consisted of pieces of cast iron riveted together. While chiselling his work, the master evidently pressed the iron over the joints and the rivets, an admirable way of concealing them so that it became impossible to see them, even with a magnifying glass. The Management of the Museum in Berlin has not yet been able to discover the joints in their work by *Leygebe*. It is, however, likely that both the other groups were made in the same way as that in Dresden, although *Leygebe* assured the Elector of Brandenburg that he had ruined his health "by pressing his body" against the "block". Height 21.5 cm.; Inv. No. IX, 2.

94 Three Bowls of Semi-Precious Stone with Mounts of Gold and Enamel

Mocha, heliotrope, jade, enamelled gold.

Left:

Bowl of Brown Mocha.

The enamel painting on the mount resembles that of works by *Georg Strauch*.

German, mid-seventeenth century, probably Nuremberg. Height 14.2 cm.; Inv. No. V, 98.

Centre:

Bowl of Heliotrope with Lid.

Most skilfully cut piece, the inside delicately finished to match the shape of the outside. The handle is formed like the cone of a stone pine and covered with translucent green enamel. The rings around the stand and around the rim of the lid are painted with flowers on a white background.

Prague (?), early seventeenth century.

Mount: Probably German, mid-seventeenth century. Height 14.5 cm.; Inv. No. V, 21.

Jade Bowl with flat fluting on the outside.

The shaft and foot are joined to the bowl with three straps, which still show traces of translucent green enamel; the straps end in grotesque masks, peering out from tulips. The shaft too is formed like a tulip; this is extremely well modelled and the flower exquisitely painted.

Early seventeenth century. Mount: mid-seventeenth century.

Height 10.7 cm.; Inv. No. V, 479.

95 Five Miniatures of Enamel

Enamel, copper, gold.

From Top to Bottom:

The Mater Dolorosa by *Ismael Mengs*, 1688–1764. Handed over to the Green Vaults in 1740 by Augustus III.

Measurements: 15.7 × 13.2 cm.; Inv. No. III, 34.

Portrait of Augustus the Strong, signed *C. Boit*, made from a portrait by *Louis de Silvestre*, formerly in the throne-room of the Dresden Palace, now in Moritzburg Castle. A miniature in body colours on paper, with the same portrait in the same size is in the Gallery of Paintings; it was probably *Boit's* sketch for his enamel work.

Between 1716 and 1720. Measurements: 12.3 × 9.7 cm.; Inv. No. III, 33.

Bears in a Mountainous Landscape by *Georg Friedrich Dinglinger*, probably from a red-chalk drawing by *Carl Andreas Ruthart* in the Cabinet of Engravings at Dresden.

Prior to 1714. Measurements 23.2 × 18.7; Inv. No. III, 42.

The Penitent Magdalene, signed *Les freres Huaut fec ano. 1698.* Enamel on gold; the frame is of silver gilt.

Measurements: 6.5 × 5.6 cm.; Inv. No. III, 35 c.

The Judgement of Salomon, signet *M. Pingart. fait.* This piece painted in enamel on gold forms the reverse side of a mirror.

French, second half of seventeenth century. Measurements: 9.4 × 8 cm.; Inv. No. III, 38/1.

96 Coffee-Set of Gold

Gold, silver, most of it gilded, enamel, diamonds, peridots and other coloured stones, pearls, ivory, lacquer, wood, glass, iron.

Made between 1697 and 1701 for Augustus the Strong by the Court Jeweller *Johann Melchior Dinglinger* and his brother the enameller *Georg Friedrich Dinglinger*. The pyramid and the two caskets at the narrow sides of the stand are of silver, everything else is of gold. This was the earliest of the master's major works and therefore the earliest work in "Dresden Baroque". In the twenties of the eighteenth century *Dinglinger* increased its height and enriched it (see J. Menzhausen *Die zwei Fassungen des Goldenen Kaffeezeugs von Johann Melchior Dinglinger* in *Jahrbuch der Staatlichen Kunstsammlungen*, Dresden, 1963–64, Dresden 1966).

Measurements: 50 × 96 × 76 cm.; Inv. No. VIII, 203.

97 Five Pieces of the Coffee-Set of Gold

Gold, enamel, glass, diamonds.

These represent the first instance in Dresden of the new "Plane Style" with Chinoiseries and ribbon-like ornaments. Only the French architect *Raymond Leplat* was using this style; as early

as 1698 he decorated the throne room and the bed-chamber in the Palace after models by *Bérain*. The blossoms in the bouquet are of coloured glass.
Height of jug 20 cm.

98 Two Goblets with Cameos

Silver gilt, rock crystal, cameos.
Left:
Goblet without Marks, South-German about 1720. On this goblet (one of two similar goblets) *Johann Heinrich Köhler* set in 1728 one hundred and sixty-eight cameos, on its companion piece one hundred and seventy-six cameos. Some of the cameos are from classical antiquity, others are Byzantine, mediaeval or Renaissance work, the majority Baroque (See E. v. Watzdorf, *J. M. Dinglinger*. Berlin, 1962, vol. 2, No. II, 352).
Height 47.5 cm.; Inv. No. V, 13.
Right:
Goblet with Lid crowned with Bust of Athena, cut in rock crystal.
Augsburg hall mark; master's mark "AP" R.840, probably of *Abraham Pratsch*, who died in 1731. About 1710–1720. Height 51 cm.; Inv. No. V, 10.

99 Basin, and Container with Lid

Silver gilt.
The Basin; the figure of Venus resting, embossed in high-relief is seen in the centre surrounded by Bacchantic scenes. Signed: *J. A. Thelot 1714*; master's mark R. 740–47. The reverse side is smooth; the Augsburg master fixed it to the front plate by soldering it on with the help of a hoop around the rim, probably so as to strengthen the basin, because the embossed high-relief work had made the silver plate exceedingly thin.
Diameter 46.9 cm.; Inv. No. IV, 5.
The Container – also referred to as a goblet – is in cast work, engraved with the figures of three Roman Emperors on horseback and with their trophies.
Augsburg hall mark; master's mark "CS", R.768. About 1700.
Height 32.5 cm.; Inv. No. IV, 188.

100 Coffee Jug with Stand and Tray

Silver gilt.
The figure of Andromeda matches the ivory figure in *Permoser's* Leipzig crucifix; the Perseus and the group of the wounded on the handles are of superior quality, probably cast from models by *Permoser*. The stand is fitted for use with a spirit-lamp.
By *Johann Jacob Irminger* (master in Dresden in 1682, died in 1724; master's mark R. 1771). 1722.
Height 39 cm.; Inv. No. IV, 251.

101 Statuette of Augustus the Strong on Horseback

Bronze.
After *Girardon*. Acquired 1716 in Paris. There are comparable works in Leningrad, Madrid and Munich. The original pedestal was lost in the Second World War, but the figures of four slaves, who sat on the volutes of the pedestal, have been preserved.
Height 105 cm.; Inv. No. IX, 67.

102 Cabinet Piece: Life's Greatest Joys

Plate of sardonyx, mocha, horn, gold, silver, gems, pearls, enamel, soap-stone.

It is the centre piece and also the largest piece of a set of three cabinet pieces, representing the three ages of man (No table set!). By the Court Jeweller *Johann Melchior Dinglinger*. According to an inscription it was finished in June 1728. Using a sketch by *Dinglinger* the sculptor *Gottlieb Kirchner*, later on modeller in the porcelain factory at Meissen, made the pedestal with the satyrs in soap-stone, and the stone-cutter *Christoph Hübner* the large cameo in sardonyx with the triumphal procession of Bacchus in high-relief.

Measurements: 18 × 16 cm. Total height 139 cm.; Inv. No. VIII, 379.

103 Detail of Plate 102: Cabinet Piece

The frame of the large sardonyx cameo is of silver gilt; the busts and the two vases are of gold and enamel.

104 Small Box for Gaming Implements

Plates of mocha, gold, silver gilt, gems, pearls, enamel.

On the lid is a very fine Chinese landscape of gold, pearls, gems and enamel. Inside the box are two small caskets with counters of silver and silver gilt, two plates for the counters in openwork of silver gilt with Chinoiseries, two packs of cards with painted Chinoiseries, a round casket of green jasper, its lid and base of enamelled gold; in this casket are three ivory dice with rubies as the spots. According to the inventory of the Jewellery Room of 1733, the box was a present from Emperor Joseph I to the wife of the Elector.

Probably from Vienna, prior to 1711. Measurements: 7.5 × 23 × 9 cm.; Inv. No. V, 594 e.

105 Vessels of Ruby-Glass

Ruby-glass, mounts of silver gilt.

The majority of the works in ruby-glass, of which there are a great number in the Collection, are of South-German origin. The principal items are the bottles with chain handles, the teapot in a mount of the late seventeenth century (to the right of the illustration) and the small cup. The conical goblet and the teapot with the Saxon-Polish coat of arms and on the reverse side the monogram "AR" in a cartouche probably came from the factory in Potsdam. In this group there are also some *Böttger*-glasses from Dresden with red flashing.

106 Two Clocks

Gold, silver gilt, gems, cameos, enamel, one pearl.

The cases of both clocks are by *Johann Heinrich Köhler*, who was born in 1669 in Langensalza, became Court Jeweller in 1718 and died in Dresden in 1736. (The Christian name of Christoph is mistakenly given to him by Sponsel and Rosenberg, No. 1791.)

Left:

Watch made by *Jehan Drouynot* of Poitiers at the beginning of the eighteenth century, and rebuilt into a pendulum-clock in 1725; the "weight" of the pendulum is a pearl.

Height 23 cm.; Inv. No. VI, 25.

Right:

Clock known as the "Hubertus Clock" because of the group shown on top of the case. By *Johann*

Gottlieb Graupner from Dresden after 1716. The rich group of figures on the top referring to hunting is influenced by *Dinglinger*.
After 1720.
Height 36 cm.; Inv. No. VI, 2.

107 Small Ornate Altar with Figure of St. Joseph

Corals, silver gilt, gems, enamel.
By *Johann Heinrich Köhler*, born 1669 in Langensalza, became Court Jeweller in 1718 and died 1736 in Dresden.
About 1730. Height 30.1 cm.; Inv. No. VI, 28.

108 Detail of Plate 110, Left: One-eyed Beggar

109 Grotesque Figurine: Halberdier

Sapphire, gold, gems, one pearl, silver gilt, enamel.
By *Ferbecq* in Frankfort on Main, R.2048 and 1777 A.
Height 10 cm.; Inv. No. VI, 81 c.

110 Three Grotesque Figurines

Baroque pearls, gold, silver gilt, gems, ivory, enamel.
Left:
One-eyed Beggar on ivory pedestal by *Jean Gerardet* of Berlin (mentioned 1700–1711), R. 1184.
Height 10.2 cm.; Inv. No. VI, 94.
Centre:
Harlequin with Mask of Negro and movable Head.
In the pedestal is a shell cameo showing under a glass-cover a mythological scene.
By *Ferbecq* in Frankfort on Main, R. 2048 and 1777 A.
Height 11.2 cm.; Inv. No. VI, 126.
Right:
Soldier with Lance and Sword.
On the enamelled cartridge pouch is the letter "W" topped by a crown.
By *Jean Gerardet* of Berlin (mentioned 1700–1711), R. 1184.
Height 9 cm.; Inv. No. VI, 81 b.

111 Four Grotesque Figurines

Baroque pearls, one large sapphire, gold, silver gilt, gems, enamel.
From Left to Right:
Dancing Dwarf after *Callot's* gnomes' parties, 1616.
By *Ferbecq* in Frankfort on Main, R. 2084 and 1777 A.
Height 8 cm.; Inv. No. VI, 97.
Hante, Court Dwarf of Augustus the Strong.
On the head is human hair. An enamelled portrait of Augustus the Strong is in the drawer of the pedestal. Described for the first time in the inventory of the Hall of Preciosities of 1733.
Height 9.5 cm.; Inv. No. VI, 16.

Happy Vintager by *Ferbecq* in Frankfort on Main, R. 2084 and 1777 A.
Height 7.9 cm.; Inv. No. VI, 100.
Merry Cook using a spit as a violin, after *Callot's* gnomes' parties, 1616. By *Ferbecq* in Frankfort on Main, R. 2048 and 1777 A. Height 12.1 cm.; Inv. No. VI, 88.

112 Grotesque Figurine: David with Head of Goliath

One pearl, gold, gems, silver gilt, marble, enamel.
Probably by a court jeweller in Dresden; mentioned for the first time in the inventory of the Hall of Preciosities of 1725.
Height 12.8 cm.; Inv. No. VI, 105.

113 Two Goblets of Ivory

Ivory, silver gilt, gems and enamel.
Left:
A *Relief* on the cup shows *Diana with Nymphs* after the hunt; a somewhat larger, but similar relief is on the goblet Inv. No. II, 30 (see Sponsel, *Das Grüne Gewölbe*, vol. IV, 1932, Pl. 14). There is also some affinity to an item in Munich (see R. Berliner, *Die Bildwerke des Bayerischen Nationalmuseums*, vol. IV, 1926, No. 189). The carving is that used in Franken, a South-German territory including Nuremberg; early eighteenth century. The *postillion d'amour* on the lid was added at the beginning of the present century. Mount by *Johann Heinrich Köhler*, born 1669 in Langensalza, became Court Jeweller in 1718 and died 1736 in Dresden. First mention of this goblet is in the inventory of 1725 of the Hall of Preciosities.
Height 35.7 cm.; Inv. No. II, 394.
Right:
The War of the Lapiths with the Centaurs is the subject of the reliefs on the cup.
Probably South-German, late seventeenth century. The mount is by *Elias Adam*, who was married in 1704 and died in 1745. Augsburg hall mark; master's mark R. 810. About 1720.
Height 47.5 cm.; Inv. No. II, 19.

114 Sitting Satyr

Box wood and four pieces of vitreous paste (imitating semi-precious stones).
The satyr was carved as supporting figure for the two heads. It is an outstanding work. Its details so closely resemble those of the "Hottentots" (Plate 115) and the "Autumn" (Plate 117) that it can be ascribed to *Balthasar Permoser*. The bust to the left was originally the end of a bauble, probably Flemish, second half of sixteenth century. The child's head resembles those by *Conrad Meit*, second quarter of sixteenth century. Mentioned for the first time in the inventory of the Hall of Preciosities of 1725.
Height 27.5 cm.; Inv. No. VII, 16.

115 Hottentot Couple

Ebony and silver gilt.
By *Balthasar Permoser*; the figures came to the Cabinet of Curiosities in 1769 from the estate of Count Brühl.
Height of both figures 18.4 cm.; Inv. Nos. VI, 237/238.

116 The Four Seasons

Ivory.

By *Balthasar Permoser*. Handed over to Augustus the Strong in 1714.
Height of all four figures 22 cm.; Inv. Nos. II, 45, 46, 48, 49.

117 Detail of "The Four Seasons": Autumn

118 Moor and Mooress as Stands

Lacquered wood, silver gilt, gems, mother of pearl.
Probably by *Balthasar Permoser* (ascribed to him by Feulner).
Dresden, early eighteenth century. Height of both figures 33 cm.; Inv. Nos. VI, 153 and 165.

119 Hercules and Omphale

Ivory.

By *Balthasar Permoser*. Signed: *Balthasar Perm: In.V.F.* There are copies of this work in the
Green Vaults, in Berlin and in Leningrad.
Height with base 30 cm.; Inv. No. II, 42.

120 Scaramouch and Columbine (?)

Ivory, partly tanned brown, silver.

By *Johann Christoph Ludwig Lücke*. Signed on the jug carried by Scaramouch *JCL Lücke* and entered
in the inventory of the Hall of Preciosities as a work by that master. The female figure, known
also as "Dancing Peasant", came to the Green Vaults as a work by *Lücke* in 1731. Originally the
figure carried a bottle not a mirror. The wooden sword of Scaramouch was lost in the Second
World War.
Height of both figures with bases 21.5 cm.; Inv. Nos. VI, 236/239.

121 Time raises fainting Art

Ivory.

By *Johann Christoph Ludwig Lücke*. Signed: *J. C. L. Lücke*. Most skilfully carved. Submitted to
Augustus III by the master in 1736 when he applied for the post of Court Sculptor.
Height without base 22 cm.; Inv. No. II, 337.

122 Three Goblets made of Nautilus Shells

Nautilus shells, mounts of silver gilt and corals.
Left:

Nautilus Goblet. By *Bernhard Quippe* in Berlin about 1700. There is no hall mark, but a master's
mark R. 1180. The model for the mount may have been made by *Balthasar Permoser*, who worked
in Berlin from 1704 to 1710.
Height 30 cm.; Inv. No. III, 189.
Centre:

Nautilus Goblet. The goblet came from the workshop of *Cornelis van Bellekin*, mid-seventeenth
century. The group forming the foot of the goblet, inclusive of the tendrils which the grotesque
figure is raising, show the influence of *Christoph Jamnitzer*. Perhaps from Nuremberg, early

seventeenth century. The mount and the crowning dragon are by the Court Jeweller *Johann Heinrich Köhler*, 1724, probably made especially for the rearranged Hall of Preciosities.

Height 42 cm.; Inv. No. III, 185.

Right:

Nautilus Goblet. Signed: *C. Bellekin f.* Second half of seventeenth century. The mount is by the Court Jeweller *Johann Heinrich Köhler*, 1724, probably made especially for the rearranged Hall of Preciosities.

Height 35 cm.; Inv. No. III, 146.

123 Cabinet Piece with Emperor-Cameo

Onyx, gold, gems, one pearl, silver gilt, agate, jasper, enamel.

By *Johann Melchior Dinglinger*, prior to 1722. The portrait of the Emperor Claudius on the classical cameo was wrongly interpreted as being Augustus and this suggested a connection with Augustus the Strong. On the plaque forming the back of the cameo are two intaglios, showing a dolphin and a capricorn, the zodiac signs under which Augustus the Strong was born. This as well as the golden stars are Baroque additions. On the top step of the pedestal is an inscription reading: *Sit gloriosum nomen tuum.* According to a description of 1722 the figure next to it is a symbol of eternity, holding a shield with the King's monogram topped by a crown. The ivory figures are by *Permoser* (ascribed to him by E. von Watzdorf).

Height 44 cm.; Inv. No. V, 1.

124 Three Vessels of Rock Crystal

Rock crystal, mounts of silver gilt with lapis lazuli.

By *Giovanni Battista Metellino* from Milan, about 1700. The Green Vaults owns more than ten works in rock crystal by this master, most of them are large. The cut is somewhat sinuous; the insertions are covered over with thinly engraved fleurons of foliage. Typical of this group of vessels are the filigree mounts.

From Left to Right:

Height 33 cm.; Inv. No. V, 312; Height 39 cm.; Inv. No. V, 315; Measurements: 21.5 × 32 × 26 cm.; Inv. No. V, 249.

125 Four Bowls of Semi-Precious Stone

Heliotrope, mocha, lapis lazuli, gold, silver gilt, gems, enamel.

From Left to Right:

Bowl of Heliotrope. On the shaft is the bust of an Emperor; the mount is of gold.

Probably from Dresden, about 1730. Height 13.7 cm.; Inv. No. V, 18.

Bowl of Mocha; with silver-gilt mount.

Dresden, about 1720. Height 14.3 cm.; Inv. No. V, 487.

Cup of Lapis Lazuli with mount of silver gilt and enamelled gold. This unusual mount comes from the workshop of *Dinglinger*. The cup too may have come from the Dresden stone-cutting mill.

Dresden, after 1700. Height 9 cm.;

Inv. No. V, 60.

Bowl of Heliotrope. The shaft formed by the bust of a negress is of black serpentine. The silver-gilt mount is set with cameos and gems.

By *Johann Heinrich Köhler*, born 1669 in Langensalza, Court Jeweller in 1718 and died in 1736 in Dresden. About 1720–1730.
Height 14.5 cm.; Inv. No. V, 25.

126 Two Cabinet Pieces: Roc and The Bath of Diana

Left:
Roc.
Sardonyx, gold, diamonds, enamel.
The cup, shaped as a dragon, came perhaps from the workshop of the brothers *Saracchi* in Milan, late sixteenth century. The mount is by *Johann Melchior Dinglinger*; the position of the wings was probably changed when the mount was made. The master referred to the seated female figure with the emblem of Augustus the Strong as "Medea".
Prior to 1709. Height 30 cm.; Inv. No. VI, 93.
Right:
The Bath of Diana.
Chalcedony, gold, silver, steel, gems, pearls, ivory, enamel.
The cup is supported by the antlers of a stag, a reference to the legend of Actaeus. The inscription in tempered steel on the pedestal also refers to it, reading: *Discretion Sert Effronterie Perd*.
Principal work by *Johann Melchior Dinglinger*, 1704. The enamelling was done by his brother *Georg Friedrich*. The ivory group has been assigned to *Balthasar Permoser*.
Height 38 cm.; Inv. No. VIII, 305.

127 Three Caskets, a Vase, a Canister and a Scent Bottle

Greenish-brown jasper, soap-stone, gold, diamonds, enamel.
All these works are by *Johann Melchior Dinglinger*.
From Left to Right:
Round Casket with Butterflies.
Late seventeenth century. Height 7 cm.; Inv. No. VI, 11.
Flat Casket with Plaited Pattern.
Late seventeenth century. Length with handles 7.1 cm.; Inv. No. VI, 7 x.
Vase of Jasper.
Between 1701 and 1708. Height with handle 15.7 cm.; Inv. No. VI, 19.
Canister for Gold Powder.
Between 1701 and 1708. Height 5.7 cm.; Inv. No. VI, 8 f.
Chinese Casket of Soap-Stone.
Mount about 1720. Height 9.3 cm.; Inv. No. VI, 13.
Scent Bottle.
Late seventeenth century. Height 6.7 cm.; Inv. No. VI, 81.

128 Three Caskets and Knob of Walking Stick

Gold and semi-precious stones.
By *Johann Christian Neuber*, born 1736, Court Jeweller about 1775, died 1808.
From Top to Bottom:
Oval Casket with Still Life of Flowers.
Measurements: 3.7 × 6.9 × 9.1 cm.; Inv. No. 1924/2.

Rectangular Casket with Pastoral Scenes.
Signed: *Neuber à Dresde 1770*.
Measurements: 3.9 × 8.5 × 6.2 cm.; Inv. No. 1933/2.
Knob of Walking Stick.
Height 4 cm.; Inv. No. 1925/3.
Round Casket with Still Life of Flowers, so-called stone-cabinet. Each of the seventy-seven semi-precious stones from Saxony which form it is numbered on its gold fillet, and inside the cabinet is a list of their places of origin. Acquired in 1911.
Diameter 7.5 cm.; Inv. No. V, 628.

129 Moor with Block of Emeralds

Emeralds in block of primitive rock, silver gilt, gems, wood, lacquer, tortoise-shell.
The block of Colombian origin came to the Cabinet of Curiosities in 1581 as a present from Emperor Rudolph II to Elector Augustus. The Moor is a work of *Balthasar Permoser*. The tortoise-shell covering of the pedestal and the tree trunk, as well as the tortoise-shell tray with Chinoiseries in piqué-work, formed by means of minute inlaid designs traced on its lower side, may well have been by *Wilhelm Krüger*. The mount came from *Dinglinger's* workshop.
As its less important companion-piece was made in 1724 by the Court Jeweller *Johann Heinrich Köhler*, it seems possible that the major work too was made especially to exhibit the famous block of emeralds in the rearranged Hall of Preciosities.
Height 63.8 cm.; Inv. No. VIII, 303.

130 Cartouche, Detail of the Cabinet Piece "Obeliscus Augustalis"

Gold, silver gilt, enamel, diamonds.
The model for the medallion with the portrait of Augustus the Strong was a relief dated 1720 by the Court Sculptor *François Coudray*. The medallion is one of *Georg Friedrich Dinglinger's* last works. The mount is by *Johann Melchior Dinglinger*. Prior to 1722.
Height 22.5 cm.; Inv. No. VIII, 350.

131 Above: Detail of the Cabinet Piece "The Apis Altar"

Sardonyx, soap-stone, intaglios, gems, silver gilt, enamel.
By *Johann Melchior Dinglinger*, 1731. It was the last of the master's major works. The cameo in sardonyx (measurements: 17.3 × 41.5 cm.) is composed of three plates. It was worked by the stone-cutter *Hübner* from a sketch by *Dinglinger*. *Hübner* also made the intaglios.
Height of the work as a whole 195 cm.; Inv. No. VIII, 202.

131 Below: Five Pieces of the Cabinet Piece "Obeliscus Augustalis"

Gold, gems, chalcedony, marble, Böttger's stoneware, ivory, enamel.
By *Johann Melchior Dinglinger*, prior to 1722. These five pieces belong to the terrace of the pedestal of the cabinet piece. The cameos were cut by *Hübner*, the clock made by the Court Watchmaker *Andreas Fichtner*, the stone-work at the "tomb of Hercules" probably by *Gottlieb Kirchner*, the vase in Böttger's stoneware was delivered from the porcelain factory at Meissen and the Polish eagle may have been carved in *Permoser's* workshop.
Height of "Hercules' tomb" 17.7 cm.; Inv. No. VIII, 350.

132 **Outside: White Elephant – Detail of the Household of the Great Mogul**
Present of Mir Miron to Aurangzeb. Height 18 cm.

132 **Cabinet Piece "The Princely Household at Delhi on the Birthday of the Great Mogul Aurangzeb"**
Gold, silver, parcel gilt, gems, pearls, enamel.
By *Johann Melchior Dinglinger* and his brothers *Georg Friedrich*, the enameller, and *Georg Christoph*, the jeweller; 1701–1708. There are one hundred and thirty-two small figures and thirty-three gifts in enamelled gold on a stage of partly gilt silver. The work is decorated with four thousand nine hundred and nine diamond roses couronnées, one hundred and sixty-four emeralds, one hundred and sixty rubies, sixteen pearls, two cameos and one sapphire. There were originally three hundred and ninety-one other precious stones and pearls, but they have been lost in the course of time.
Aurangzeb reigned from 1658 to 1707. He was considered a most wealthy and mighty sovereign. For his work *Dinglinger* mainly used illustrations of travel-descriptions and also literature on India dealing with ethnology, fine art and archaeology. His work displays his encyclopaedic knowledge and probably represents the first large piece of Chinoiserie in Germany.
Measurements: 58 × 142 × 114 cm.; Inv. No. VIII, 204.

133 **Detail of the Household of the Great Mogul: Wall of the Throne**

134 **Relief Portrait in Mother of Pearl of Augustus the Strong on Horseback**
Mother of pearl, mounted in silver gilt.
Görlitz hall mark; master's mark "IAK". Mentioned for the first time in the inventory of the Hall of Preciosities of 1733. Height 34 cm.; Inv. No. VI, 80.

135 **Single Pieces from a Jewellery Set with Cornelians**
Aigrette to be worn on hat, formed by a spray of four hundred and eight brilliants in a silver-gilt mount. From *Dinglinger's* workshop, prior to 1719. Inv. No. VIII, 233.
Round Snuff-Box representing the celestial globe; gold and ninety brilliants. From *Dinglinger's* workshop, 1719. Inv. No. VIII, 238.
Large Hunting Knife with three hundred and twenty-seven brilliants; from *Dinglinger's* workshop. Inv. No. VIII, 240.
Small Hunting Knife, hilt mounted in gold, from *Dinglinger's* workshop. Inv. No. VIII, 242.
Hunting Crop with handle decorated with gold-wire, one hundred and thirty brilliants and one ruby. Ascribed to *Johann Melchior Dinglinger*, prior to 1719. Inv. No. VIII, 243.
Oblong Jewellery Etui decorated with gold-wire and seventy-eight brilliants. Ascribed to *Johann Melchior Dinglinger*, prior to 1719. Inv. No. VIII, 230.
Badge of the Order of the Golden Fleece with one hundred and thirty-five brilliants. After 1719. Inv. No. VIII, 241.
Tall Hunting Snuff-Box with one hundred and four brilliants, the more precious stones set with wreaths of smaller ones. 1721. Inv. No. VIII, 235.
Watch, the case decorated with precious stones. Probably from *Dinglinger's* workshop, 1721. Inv. No. VIII, 234.
Also: Three *Buckles*.

136 Single Pieces from a Jewellery Set with Sapphires

Badge of the Polish Order of the White Eagle with fifteen sapphires and twenty-nine brilliants. By *Johann Melchior Dinglinger*, between 1704 and 1713. Inv. No. VIII, 160.

Sword with sixty-five sapphires and three hundred and eighty-nine diamonds. By *Johann Melchior Dinglinger*, about 1700 and again about 1721. Inv. No. VIII, 165.

Ornaments from Sword-Belt, consisting of ten pieces. By *Johann Melchior Dinglinger*, about 1700 and again about 1721. Inv. Nos. VIII, 149–151 and 156–159.

Hat-Ornament with one high and three table-cut sapphires and ninety-seven diamonds. Inv. No. VIII, 161.

Also: Two *Buckles* and two *Buttons*.

137 Single Pieces from a Jewellery Set with Brilliants

Star of the Polish Order of the White Eagle with brilliants and rubies. In the centre is a brilliant of $19^5/_8$ carat.
Inv. No. VIII, 23.

Sword with Scabbard decorated with one thousand, eight hundred and ninety-eight brilliants, the largest of which weighs $9^4/_8$ carat. Inv. No. VIII, 29.

Clasp to be worn on hat, the largest stone of which weighs $9^3/_8$ carat. Inv. No. VIII, 26.

Clasp to be worn on hat with green brilliant, weighing 40 carat. This stone was bought in 1742 in Leipzig for 200,000 Thaler, and set by *Johann Friedrich Dinglinger* into a badge of the Order of the Golden Fleece. In 1746 the jeweller *Pallard* from Geneva – later on Court Jeweller in Dresden – set it together with the large brilliant of $48^4/_8$ carat from the shoulder knot (in the illustration to the left of the green brilliant) into a new badge of the Golden Fleece. But in 1768 the jeweller *Diessbach* dismantled *Pallard's* badge and used its two principal stones for the jewellery pieces at present in the Collection, that is for the clasp to be worn on the hat and for the shoulder-knot. The ropes of brilliants are by *Diessbach*, the bouquet-like arrangement around the two large stones by *Pallard*.
Inv. No. VIII, 30.

Shoulder-Knot (see above description of clasp to be worn on hat). Inv. No. VIII, 25.

Also: One pair of *Clasps* to be worn on shoe, two pairs of *Cuff-Links* and two *Shirt-Buttons*, each of the latter with a large yellow brilliant, the larger one weighing $18^2/_8$ carat.

138 Single Pieces from a Tortoise-Shell Set

This set was made for Augustus the Strong by *Peter* (?) *Triquet*, an Englishman; it has been ascertained that he worked at it from 1721 to 1728. The decoration in brilliants is by the Court Jeweller *Johann Heinrich Köhler*. There exists an account for it dating from 1731. The whole set is detailed in the inventory of the Jewellery Room of 1733. In the years 1824 and 1827 the Court Jeweller *Ploedterl* removed most of the larger stones from this set to enlarge with them the Brilliant Set.

Sword, still decorated with two hundred and forty-three brilliants. Inv. No. VIII, 220.

Hunting Knife, still decorated with two hundred and ninety-one brilliants. Inv. No. VIII, 221.

Hunting Crop, still decorated with four hundred and forty-one brilliants. Inv. No. VIII, 224.

Badge of the Polish Order of the White Eagle, retaining all its sixty-five brilliants. Inv. No. VIII, 215.

Star of the Polish Order of the White Eagle, retaining all its one hundred and seventy-three brilliants. Inv. No. VIII, 224a.

Badge of the Order of the Golden Fleece, retaining all its thirty-five brilliants. Inv. No. VIII, 214.

Snuff-Box. Inv. No. VIII, 217.

Watch, marked on dial "*Cabrier* London". The piqué-work does not seem to be by *Triquet*, yet is probably from London. Inv. No. VIII, 219.

Note Book, retaining all its hundred and twenty-five brilliants, forty diamonds, sixteen emeralds, six rubies, one opal and one piece of rock crystal. Inv. No. VIII, 218.

Also: Eight *Buttons* each for coat and waistcoat.

139 Single Pieces from a Jewellery Set with Emeralds

Badge of the Polish Order of the White Eagle, decorated with sixteen emeralds and with brilliants. Inv. No. VIII, 142.

Badge of the Order of the Golden Fleece with three emeralds and seventy-two brilliants. Inv. No. VIII, 135.

Sword with ninety emeralds and two hundred and twenty brilliants. By *Johann Friedrich Dinglinger*, 1737. Inv. No. VIII, 145.

Hunting Knife with hilt of agate, mounted in gold and with golden cross guard; decoration: nine emeralds and eighty-one brilliants. By *Johann Melchior Dinglinger*, first decade of eighteenth century. Inv. No. VIII, 144.

Clasp to be worn on hat, decorated with four emeralds and sixty-seven brilliants. Inv. No. VIII, 137.

Belt for Hunting Knife; four of its still extant nine parts are: a buckle with three convex emeralds and fifty-three brilliants, and three aglets (on illustration between sword and hunting knife). By *Georg Christoph Dinglinger*, prior to 1719. Inv. No. VIII, 133.

Also: *Knob of Walking-Stick* and three large *Emeralds* mounted in gold.

140/141 Single Pieces from a Jewellery Set with Brilliants and Pearls

Two hundred and twenty-eight *Oriental Pearls on Four Strings.* Inv. No. VIII, 32.

One hundred and seventy-seven *Saxon Pearls* from the White Elster on *One String*; originally these too were on four strings. Inv. No. VIII, 33.

Large Breast Knot with fifty-one large and six hundred and eleven smaller brilliants; the large stone in the centre weighs $21^6/_8$ carat. Made 1782 by the jeweller *A. G. Globig.* Inv. No. VIII, 36.

Necklace of thirty-eight brilliants set à jour; the drop-shaped pendant weighs $29^7/_8$ carat. In the eighteenth century this necklace was made up of twenty-five stones, but it was reset and enlarged in 1819, and reached its present length through a further resetting in 1824 by the Court Jeweller *Ploedterl.* Inv. No. VIII, 38.

Hair Ornament. On a golden eagle decorated with black enamel hangs a drop-shaped diamond of $17^1/_8$ carat, thought to be one of the purest diamonds in the world. Earliest authentic representation of it is on a portrait of 1750 of Queen Maria Josepha. The ornament probably is by *Johann Melchior Dinglinger.* Inv. No. VIII, 37.

Also: A pair of *Earrings*, two *Pendants*, three pieces of *Hair Ornament*, a *Clasp to hold a Muff*, ten *Hairpins* (single brilliants set à jour), and forty-five *Rings*, all from the eighteenth century, among them some with blue, brown, yellow or pink diamonds.

142 Single Pieces from a Jewellery Set with Rubies

Badge of the Polish Order of the White Eagle, decorated with sixteen rubies and four hundred and eighty brilliants. By the jeweller *Jordan*, 1744. Inv. No. VIII, 123.

Star of the Polish Order of the White Eagle, decorated with two hundred and sixty-eight rubies and three hundred and eighty-five brilliants. Was in the Collection in 1733. Inv. No. VIII, 121.

Sword with one hundred and twelve rubies and four hundred and one brilliants. Inv. No. VIII, 125.

Hat-Knot with twelve spinel-rubies and ninety-six brilliants. By *Johann Friedrich Dinglinger*, 1736. Inv. No. VIII, 124.

Badge of the Order of the Golden Fleece with three spinel-rubies and seventy brilliants. Inv. No. VIII, 122.

Two Pendants made of spinel-rubies of 59^4/$_8$ carat and 48 carat respectively; the mounts are of gold, topped by crowns formed of brilliants. Both pendants were acquired in 1740. Inv. Nos. VIII, 119 and 120.

Snuff-Box of gold with twenty-five rubies and one hundred and eighty-nine brilliants. Signed: "*Gouers Paris*". In the Collection in 1733. Inv. No. VIII, 127.

Also: Three *Buckles* and two *Shirt Buttons*.

143 Single Pieces from a Jewellery Set with Diamond-Rosettes

Badge of the Order of the Golden Fleece, decorated with three garnets from Bohemia, the largest of 46^6/$_8$ carat, and three hundred and eighteen brilliants. In 1737 *Johann Friedrich Dinglinger* was given ten, mostly large Bohemian garnets, to use them in badges of the Order of the Golden Fleece. Inv. No. VIII, 6.

Badge of the Order of the Polish White Eagle with two hundred and twenty-five diamonds, the largest 3^7/$_8$ carat. Inv. No. VIII, 18.

Star of the Polish Order of the White Eagle with two hundred and twenty-five diamonds, the largest 11^4/$_8$ carat. The cross is made of rubies. Inv. No. VIII, 17.

Sword with seven hundred and eighty diamonds, the largest 8^1/$_8$ carat. Inv. No. VIII, 16.

Shoulder-Knot with two hundred and thirty-six diamonds, the largest 40^6/$_8$ carat. Inv. No. VIII, 11.

Clasp to be worn on hat with one hundred and eighteen diamonds, the largest 24^3/$_8$ carat. Inv. No. VIII, 10.

Pair of Buckles for shoes with one hundred and four diamonds. Inv. No. VIII, 12.

Badge of the Order of the Golden Fleece with three opals on red foil and one hundred and one diamonds. Inv. No. VIII, 2.

The classification of the master's marks "R". refers to M. Rosenberg: *Der Goldschmiede Merkzeichen*. 4 vols., 3rd edition, Frankfort on Main, 1922–1928.

INDEX OF NAMES

In addition to the photographs by Gerhard Reinhold photographs were used from
Klaus G. Beyer, Weimar: Plates 16, 21, 56, 64, 66, 79, 119, 129, 132, 133
Deutsche Fotothek Dresden: Illustrations on pp. 13, 17, 40, 41, 44, 45, 49
Institut und Museum für die Geschichte der Stadt Dresden: Illustrations on pp. 21, 24, 25, 36, 37
Staatliche Kunstsammlungen Dresden (Pfauder): Illustrations on pp. 20, 48

ILLUSTRATIONS

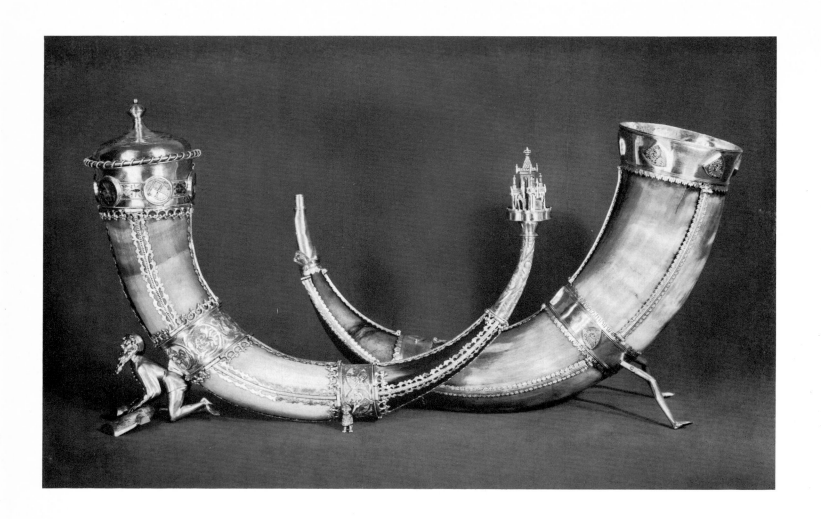

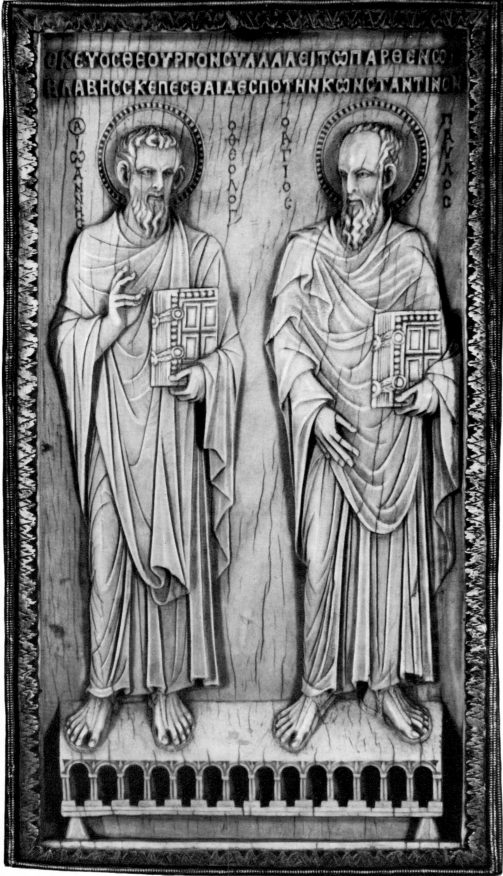

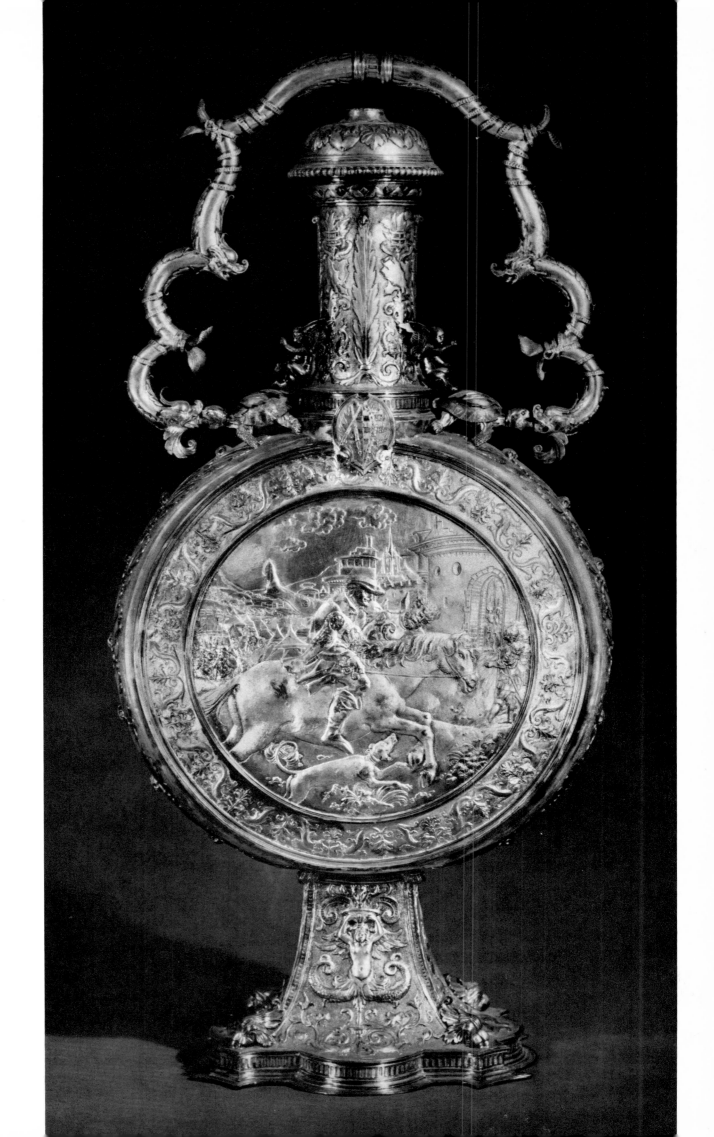

30

34

48

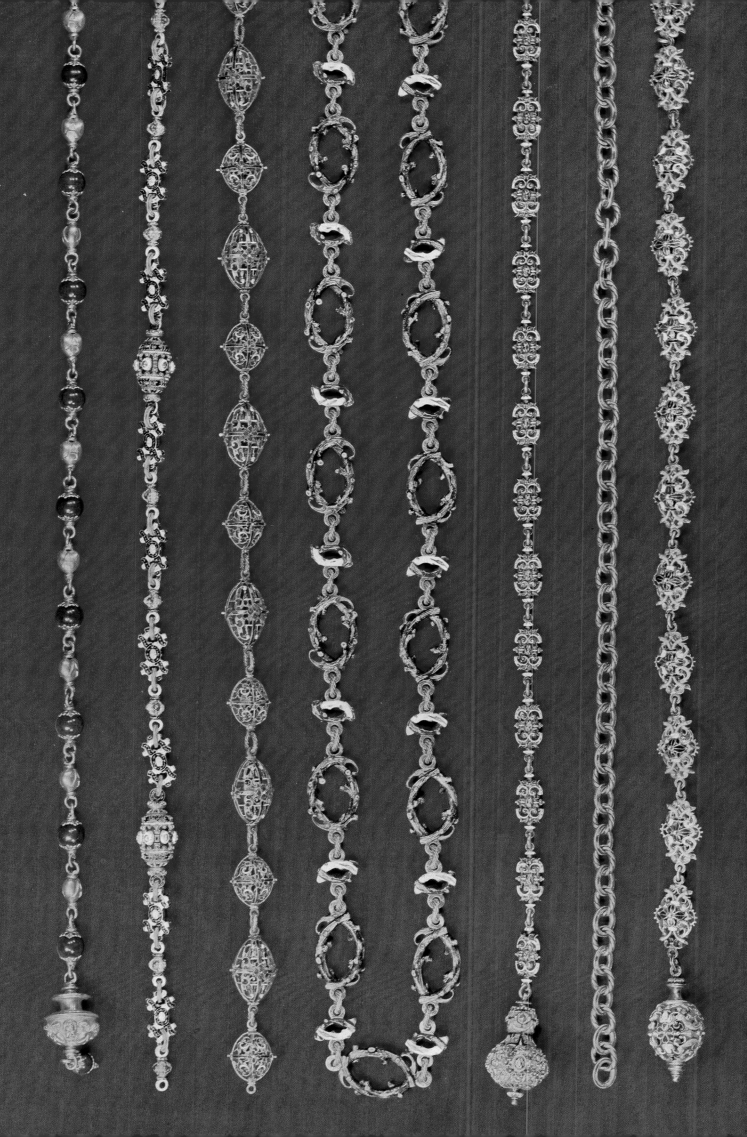

70

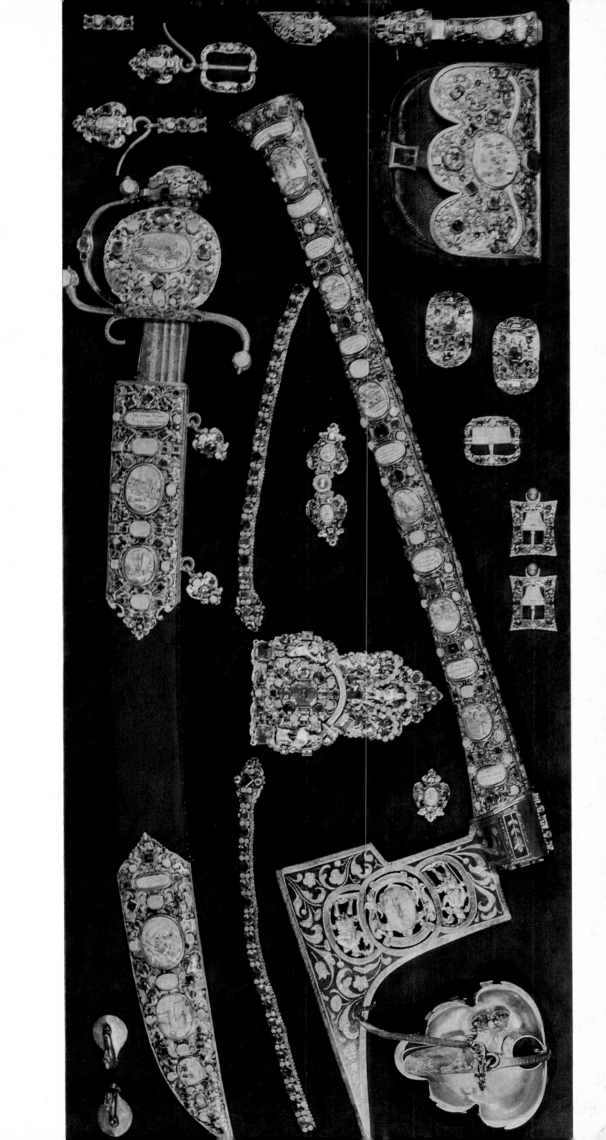

88

96

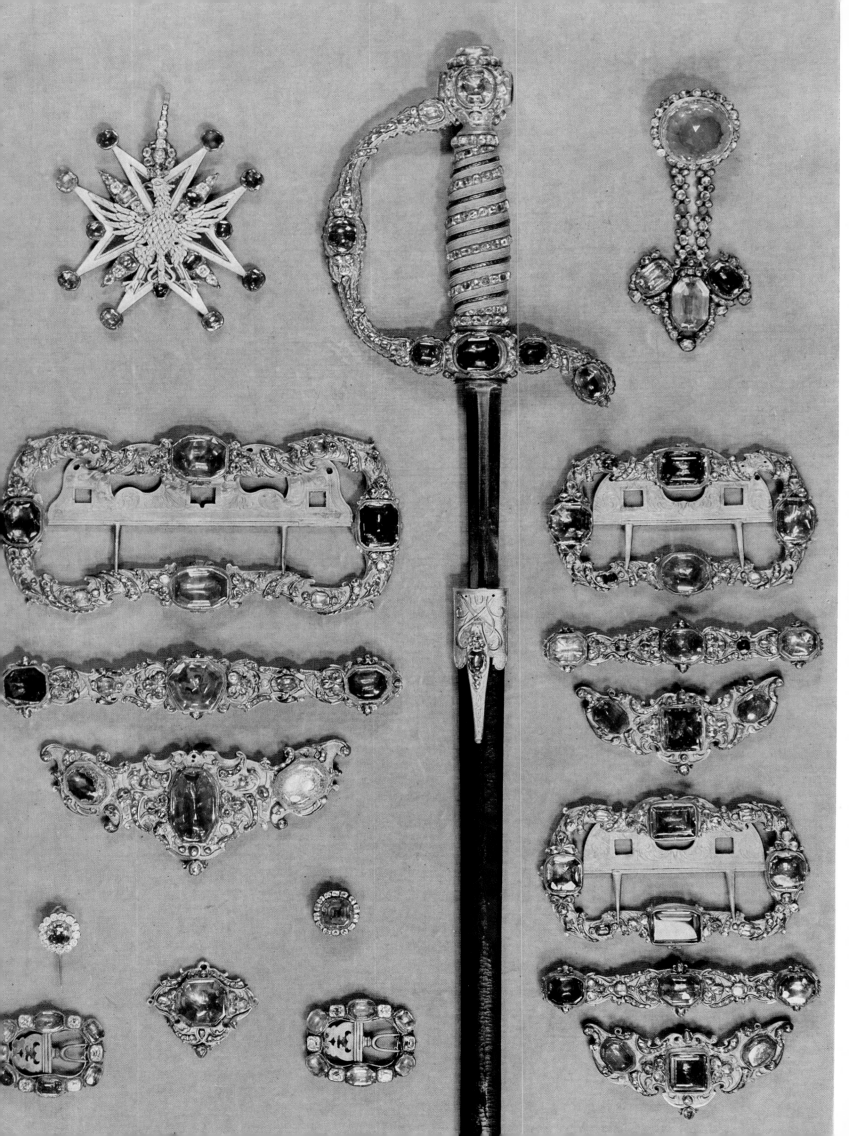

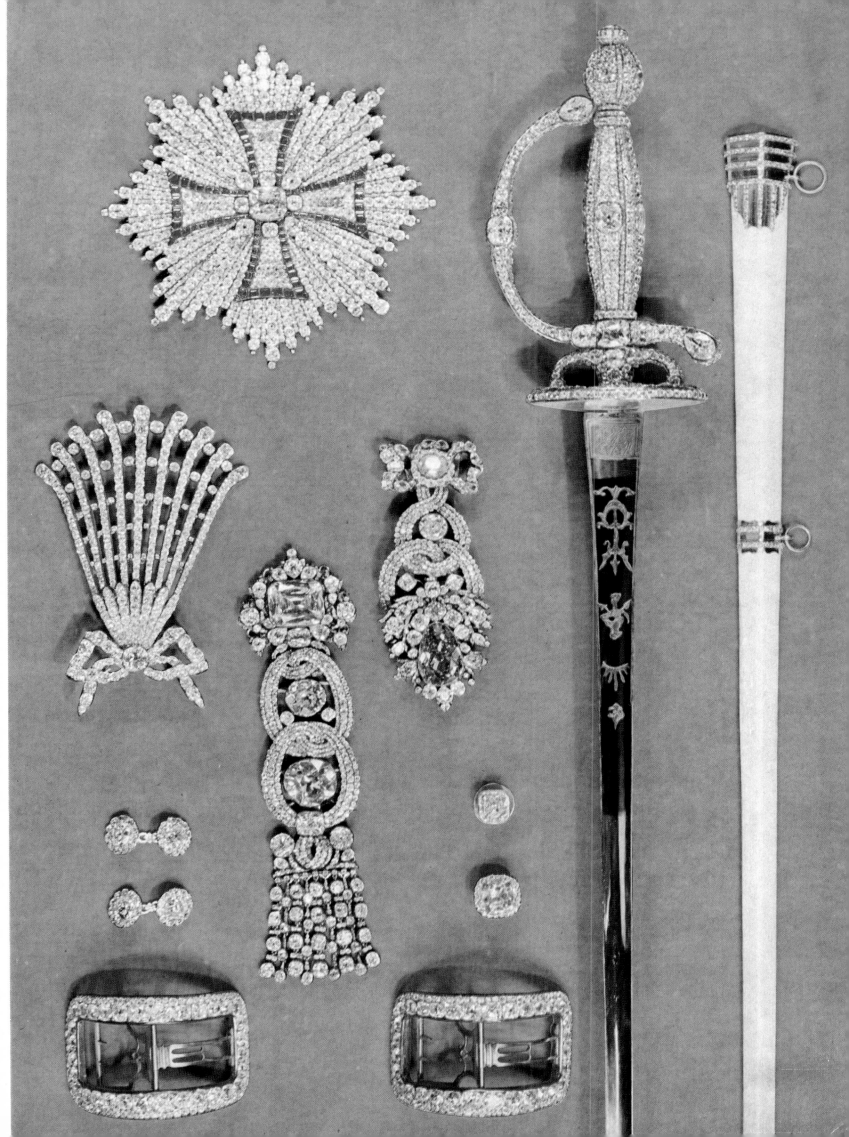

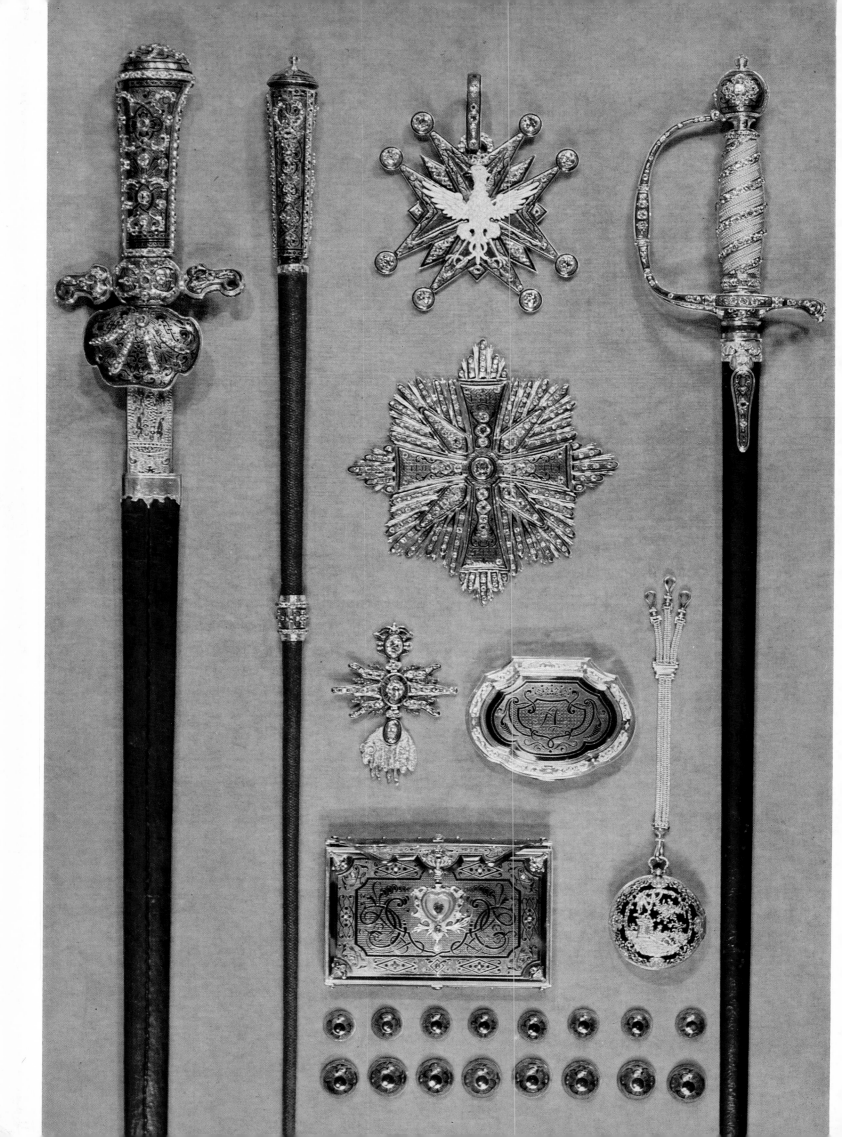